THE *evolving* FEMININE
ballet body

THE *evolving* FEMININE
ballet body

Pirkko Markula
& Marianne I. Clark, Editors

THE UNIVERSITY OF ALBERTA PRESS

Published by

THE UNIVERSITY OF ALBERTA PRESS
Ring House 2
Edmonton, Alberta, Canada   T6G 2E1
www.uap.ualberta.ca

LIBRARY AND ARCHIVES CANADA CATALOGUING IN PUBLICATION

The evolving feminine ballet body / Pirkko Markula &
Marianne I. Clark, editors.

Includes bibliographical references and index.
Issued in print and electronic formats.
ISBN 978-1-77212-334-0 (softcover). —ISBN 978-1-77212-354-8 (PDF).
—ISBN 978-1-77212-352-4 (EPUB). —ISBN 978-1-77212-353-1 (Kindle)

1. Ballet—Social aspects. 2. Human body—Social aspects.
I. Markula, Pirkko, 1961–, editor II. Clark, Marianne I., 1976–, editor

GV1787.E96 2018   792.8   C20179058681
                              C2017-905869-X

First edition, first printing, 2018.
First printed and bound in Canada by Houghton Boston Printers,
    Saskatoon, Saskarchewan.
Copyediting and proofreading by Joanne Muzak.
Indexing by Adrian Mather.

The University of Alberta Press is
committed to protecting our natural
environment. As part of our efforts,
this book is printed on Enviro Paper: it
contains 100% post-consumer recycled
fibres and is acid- and chlorine-free.

The University of Alberta Press
gratefully acknowledges the support
received for its publishing program
from the Government of Canada, the
Canada Council for the Arts, and the
Government of Alberta through the
Alberta Media Fund.

Canada Canada Council Conseil des Arts   Alberta
for the Arts du Canada   Government

*For the Orchesis Dance Program
at the University of Alberta
and all dancers whose passion
moves them to continue dancing
no matter how small or big
the stage.*

CONTENTS

ACKNOWLEDGEMENTS

We would like to thank all of our contributors who made the publication of this book possible. We also thank the University of Alberta Press staff whose assistance guided us through the final editing and publishing stages. In addition, we would like to offer a word of personal thanks.

PIRKKO MARKULA: I would like to thank the Social Sciences and Humanities Research Council for providing funding that made writing Chapter 2 possible. In addition, this funding has significantly supported the publication of this book. I am very much indebted to Mariel Day, whose careful editing and care for details greatly enhanced the final manuscript. I am also grateful to have colleagues at my faculty whose passion for dance was an inspiration for this book: Thank you, Tamara Bliss and the rest of the Initial 6 Research Group Dancers! Finally, as always, I extend my thanks to Jim Denison for his enduring intellectual and personal support.

MARIANNE I. CLARK: I would like to thank the Social Sciences and Humanities Research Council for supporting my dissertation research and therefore making Chapter 4 possible. I would also like to thank my colleagues and peers at the University of Alberta for their invaluable support, inspiration, and shared passion for movement, which deeply enriched the research informing this project. My love for dance was nourished by my dance teacher, Patricia McLeod, who extended such care to her students and to whom I am forever grateful. Finally, I give my thanks to Sean Stolp, whose unwavering support and endless stream of morning coffee keeps me moving, dancing, and writing.

PREFACE

The Evolving Feminine Ballet Body is a collection of scholarly writings by a group of researchers with a curiosity, passion, and what we consider a complicated love for ballet. We share an ongoing preoccupation with the ballet body, at once evocative, problematic, awe-inspiring, and political, and how it shapes and is shaped by contemporary culture. This preface stories the book's inception and outlines what we hope this collection achieves, provokes, and brings to future discussions and inquiry.

It is this cultural moment, in which dance is becoming increasingly visible in multiple social and cultural spaces, that prompted this collection of essays by a group of faculty members and graduate students in the Faculty of Physical Education and Recreation at the University of Alberta. We come with a wide range of dance backgrounds and, in some ways, accidentally stumbled on a shared interest of researching ballet. As one of the editors for this collection, Pirkko learned about other contributors' interest in analyzing contemporary forms of ballet in various ways. For example, she still vividly remembers attending a ballet class taught by Jodie. The class was preceded by a heated discussion of the televised reality show *So You Think You Can Dance* and its representation of dance and dancers, as well as the increased visibility and acceptance of dance in Canadian society. Pirkko was so intrigued that she obtained a Social Sciences and Humanities Research Council grant to study the show. Jodie became interested in pursuing a master's degree at the faculty to examine how to make recreational ballet classes safer and more meaningful. Kate discovered ballet by accident when she was defining the sample for her PHD dissertation research on children's sport books. When she searched for the most popular books, to her surprise, six books of ballet emerged in her top thirty list. Although surprised by the number of ballet books, Kate then immersed herself into the world of ballet to further understand why these books sell so well.

Other contributors have an established and ongoing relationship with dance, but were curious about ballet in particular. Carolyn, like Jodie, Kelsie, Lindsay, and Marianne, danced with the Faculty of Physical Education and Recreation dance group, Orchesis, to continue her dance career after her private studio training. She felt strongly about the positive impact of this dance group, which provides continued opportunities for adult dancers with a focus on contemporary dance. Carolyn was particularly interested in how her fellow dancers with a ballet background found this new environment. Marianne was further curious about how recreational dancers made sense of their ballet bodies, as her own experiences of studying ballet as an adolescent girl did not always fit with themes that emerge in the literature. Pirkko also invited Kelsie and Lindsay to contribute a chapter to this collection after learning about their attempts to develop accessible ways of including ballet technique in their inclusive dance classes with Solidance Inclusive Recreation.

Collectively, we hold a variety of academic backgrounds and professional interests encompassing kinesiology, occupational therapy, disability studies, cultural studies, dance studies, and feminist poststructuralist studies. As a group that has danced, learned, taught, and researched together, it became increasingly apparent that our academic interests in physically active bodies, and our personal involvement with and practice of ballet, were inextricably linked. As social scientists and qualitative researchers, we observed ballet exceeding the boundaries of its previously appointed home within elite performance art into the realm of the popular imagination: It is now an increasingly popular physical cultural and fitness practice in which girls and women (and boys and men) of all ages participate, and is a form of widely consumed entertainment. We were interested in these multiple representations and experiences not captured by the enduring image of the prima ballerina in her tulle tutu and pink satin pointe shoes. We wondered about those ballet bodies that fill recreational dance classes, integrated dance classes, popular television shows, and fitness magazines, to name a few. We wondered about ballet bodies of diverse ages, backgrounds, and abilities, and how that diversity is (or is not) represented. We wondered about the social consequences of the renewed cultural interest for those who practice, teach, and consume ballet. In this book, we aim to capture some of the ways the ballet body continues to evolve alongside the shifting meanings, forms, and iterations of ballet in the current social and historical conditions.

We suggest the ballet body is important to examine *now* because we live in a world where all bodies face increased scrutiny and pressure to comply with stringent and often unrealistic ideals of beauty that are linked, often problematically, to notions of Western citizenship and morality. Contemporary bodies are also monitored and measured in various and increasingly insidious ways in the name of health, and subjected to and shaped by prolific forms of medical expertise. Therefore, we argue that the ballet body steps onto the proverbial stage under a unique and complex constellation of social conditions.

At a time when bodies are understood as complex material, social, and cultural entities, we consider an interdisciplinary faculty, like the Faculty of Physical Education and Recreation, a good place to start such an inquiry. Although often located within performing arts or social sciences, dance research, we believe, can strongly benefit from the type of research community we have shared within our faculty at the University of Alberta. We hope that this collection further increases the visibility and appreciation for dance research done in interdisciplinary environments.

While we acknowledge that these essays may provoke as many questions as they seek to answer, we believe this is an appropriate overture to open up important lines of inquiry around the ballet body and its intersections and entanglements with culture, power relations, gender, disability, movement mechanics, and the dancing body. In conclusion, we believe and hope this collection of essays presents a timely exploration of the multiplicity of the ballet body as it is both represented and experienced. For, like the ballet body itself, meaning and knowledge are never fixed or still.

INTRODUCTION

Pirkko Markula and Marianne I. Clark

Although ballet has traditionally been relatively invisible within the popular imagination, it appears to be edging its way into the mainstream. Through films such as *Black Swan*, popular TV reality shows *Dancing with the Stars* and *So You Think You Can Dance*, and even fitness forms such as the barre class, which fuses ballet barre workouts with exercise, ballet has become somewhat of a craze. Consequently, in small but notable ways, ballet is expanding its presence in popular and physical culture, stepping steadily out of its marginal, high-art status into the mainstream. We believe that it is timely to engage in scholarly inquiry that aims to imagine ballet, broadly and theoretically, in contemporary society.

To date, ballet has received comparatively little attention outside of the field of dance studies, which tends to focus on "high art" (Boyd, 2004), theatrical ballet. In this book, we invite further study into the myriad ways ballet reflects and upholds value systems as well as how it might shape, disrupt, and provoke such systems in popular culture. We specifically note that ballet still has a strong attraction for many Canadian girls and women who do not strive to be professional dancers but nonetheless engage seriously in dance. For example, in Edmonton alone, there are over 50 dance studios and schools that offer classes to dancers with a range of experience, and it is estimated over 625,000 Canadian girls participate in dance classes (Solutions Research Group, 2014).

Given the many faces of ballet in our contemporary culture, this collection aims to provide insights into the significance of ballet to community, popular culture, and dance scholarship. We also aim to answer a call for increased social analysis of ballet. A strong dance community at the University of Alberta—students, researchers, choreographers, and performers—is currently conducting a significant amount of research on contemporary issues of ballet, and thus can provide a unique local perspective to enrich the broader cultural narratives of ballet. To provide further context for the local work in this collection, we reflect upon the existing research on the current context of professional, high-art ballet.

The Evolving Image of the Feminine Ballet Body

There is an established body of research that traces the history of ballet since its emergence in the sixteenth century (Karthas, 2012) as well as feminist research that maps the contemporary experiences in ballet. To specifically situate the research generated in our collection, we approach the rich earlier research through several enduring binaries that continue to characterize the image of the ballerina and the experiences of dancing ballet in current society. We follow Karthas (2012) to observe that ballet has evolved alongside the general cultural and social developments of each era of its existence:

> Ballet was born in the royal court, professionalized in the state theatre, nurtured by Romanticism, degenerated by consumerism and commercialism, and resurrected by modernism (via a flourishing Russian ballet). Through-

out the ages, the profession of ballet has carried with it various political and symbolic meanings. (961)

To begin, we trace ballet to the court of Louis XIV in France where it was used as a part of the king's ruling strategy. This discussion illustrates the development of ballet as an art form within the binary of technical prowess and expressiveness.

Ballet as a Technical or Expressive Art Form

In the court of Louis XIV, ballet was loaded with political meanings of male dominance exhibited visibly by the king himself. To add to the power of ballet, in 1661, Louis XIV founded the Académie Royale de Danse (later known as the Paris Opéra) that established technical principles of dance to improve dance instruction and to train professional dancers to perform "to imitate the grace of the aristocratic body on stage" (Karthas, 2012, 962). At this point, the male dancers performed the female roles "en travest" (Karthas, 2012, 962). When dance turned into a professional theatre art, women increasingly joined the ranks of professional dancers. A permanent dance company of ten men and ten women and a school, open also to boys and girls from poor families, were established in 1713 (Karthas, 2012).

The term *ballet* was popularized by the Opéra chief dance master and choreographer Jean-Baptiste Noverre. He started favouring the so-called *ballet d'action*, designed to "copy nature faithfully and to delineate the emotions upon the stage" (cited in Karthas, 2012, 962), instead of the demi-character style that required more technical virtuosity (Eliot, 2007). The expressive *ballet d'action* initiated one of the enduring binaries of ballet: Is expressiveness or technical virtuosity essential for ballet as a dance form? This binary also began to reinforce the gender differentiation in ballet: women were thought to be naturally more expressive than men, who, in Louis XIV's court, exclusively used ballet to exhibit their masculine power. The emphasis on expressiveness, however, opened the door for the first female dance celebrities such as the Italian *ballet d'action* star Marie Camargo.

The nature of ballet changed substantially with the political changes of nineteenth-century France. "Once chilvalric and noble of ideal of masculinity," the male ballet dancer who was strongly associated with displays of aristocratic masculinity was now judged as "dangerously effeminate," "clumsy," "indecent," even "monstrous" (Karthas, 2012, 965). In this political climate, the expressive ballerina was lifted to centre stage and the men were assigned to supporting background characters through which they, nevertheless, exhibited great strength, speed, and technical ability.

While the expressive style was the foundation for the Romantic ballerina in the early 1800s, technicality became re-emphasized in imperialist Russia where the ballerinas began to emulate the more technical- and strength-oriented Italian Cecchetti style at the turn of the twentieth century (Eliot, 2007). After the revolution in Russia, the Ballets Russes (1909–1929), which took the great Russian ballet tradition abroad, continued to assign female dancers more athletic movement vocabulary.[1] The Ballets Russes further disrupted the traditional gender images by bringing the (openly sexualized) male dancer back to the centre stage of ballet and making overt and covert allusions to male homosexuality. In this process, men (e.g., commisario Sergei Diaghilev and star dancer Vaslav Nijinsky) also tended to dominate the Ballets Russes, leaving the achievements of the female stars (e.g., Tamara Karsavina and Bronislava Nijinska) almost invisible (Eliot, 2007). Nevertheless, the technical requirements initiated in the Ballets Russes performances were perfected by one of its male members, George Balanchine, who had a major influence on ballet in the United States.

With the help and determination of American ballet impresario Lincoln Kirstein, Balanchine founded the New York City Ballet and acted as its director from 1948 to the early 1980s (Laemmli, 2015; Morris, 2005). Balanchine's signature style of modernist neoclassism (Harris, 2007; Kowal, 2014; Morris, 2005) exemplified formalist, non-representational modernism through the optical illusion of grace and weightlessness. Instead of the expressiveness of the Ballets Russes or the narratives of neoclassical ballet, Balanchine emphasized the importance of technique (Morris, 2005) in his minimalist ballets, which were performed without elaborate costuming or set design to accentuate human movement, not emotionality or expressiveness, as the most central aspect of ballet art. The image of the American ballerina playing "down emotional qualities for control, regularity and precision" (Morris, 2005, 35) persists in the current popular context of ballet. In her analysis of the reality show *So You Think You Can Dance, Canada* in Chapter 2, Pirkko Markula explains that the ballerinas, while judged to be technically superb, are considered lacking the ability to express emotions required for winning performances on the show.

While the Romantic and neoclassical ballets, as well as iconic works by the Ballets Russes and Balanchine, remain beloved parts of ballet repertoire throughout the world, new types of ballet choreography continue to evolve. Contemporary ballets expand ballet's movement repertoire, sets, stage design, costuming, and lighting (Alterowich, 2014). Among the most acclaimed contemporary ballet choreographers is British choreographer William Forsythe, who emphasized the ballet movement in favour of expression.

Drawing from the poststructuralist scholarship of Roland Barthes, Jacques Derrida, and Michel Foucault (Briginshaw, 2001; Franko, 2011a, 2011b; Hammond, 2013), Forsythe wanted to disrupt the coherent narrative of ballet. Unlike Balanchine, Forsythe believed that through his "postclassical analysis" (Hammond, 2013, 128) and consequent "recoordination of ballet" (127), he was able to critique the institution of ballet, its discursive formation, and its Europeanist roots. Particularly his balletic ballets (e.g., *Firstext, Steptext*) underscored a previously invisible or subjugated knowledge of ballet as an institution, and disrupted its traditional practice in several ways. Of particular relevance to our collection, Forsythe, who was critical of the disciplined ballet body, advocated new movement practices. According to him, an emphasis on proprioception—ballet's physical language—provided an alternative to the logocentricism of contemporary society, and thus an alternative way of sensing one's self. One of the authors in this collection, Jodie Vandekerhove in Chapter 6, continues to trace possible subjugated knowledge embedded in ballet movement when, using Foucauldian framework, she explores ethical training practices for a grassroots-level, beginners' ballet class.

Like Forsythe, some male modern dance choreographers such as Mark Morris (*The Hard Nut*)[2] and Matthew Bourne (*Swan Lake*, *Sleeping Beauty*) have "reworked" (Alterowich, 2014, 341) the neoclassical ballets with their own movement vocabulary, but retained the main storylines. These versions, like some of Forsythe's work or the Ballets Russes, challenge the traditional gender politics of ballet by reassigning the roles or introducing queer relationships to previously heterosexual plots.

Ballet as an art form has evolved through changing emphases on expression and technicality. However, it is the male choreographers who have led the development from the *ballet d'action* to the contemporary reworkings of ballet. As Alterowich (2014) points out, in the hands of these men, "ballet has become a powerful tool for identifying and locating a kind of covert or implicit male queerness often associated with effeminacy or a sexualized display of the male body" (340). Women's queer perspectives are less visible (Alterowich, 2014) and, some exceptions notwithstanding, the conventional standards of femininity have shaped the ballerina's body through the binary of ethereal elegance and open sexualization.

The Voluptuous or Ethereal Feminine Ballet Body

In the early nineteenth century, famous ballets such as *La Sylphide* (1832) and *Giselle* (1841) embraced the Romantic themes of "beauty, passion, nature, the supernatural, exoticism, and the power of love" (Karthas, 2012, 971). In this era, the star ballerina was celebrated as the signification of beauty and elegance, and her visuality, instead of her technical prowess, became of primary importance. For example, Théophile Gautier, an influential French ballet critic between 1830 and 1870, declared that "[it] must not be forgotten that the first quality a dancer should possess is that of beauty" (cited in Karthas, 2012, 972). As a result, his evaluation focused on the looks of the ballerina—her head, forehead, nose, bosom, arms, and legs—to emphasize "the physical voluptuousness and beauty of woman" (cited in Karthas, 2012, 972). The narrative themes, technique, and clothing (Karthas, 2012; Laemmli, 2015) of the Romantic ballet further reinforced this ideal—the innocent, shapely young woman passively suffering from romantic (recruited or unfulfilled) love now exemplified the beautiful feminine body. Displayed as either an ethereal supernatural being (a sylph in *La Sylphide*) or a woman who, victim of tragic love with mortal men, is turned into a supernatural being (a wili in *Giselle*), the ballerina's otherworldliness was enhanced by two important inventions that remain the quintessential ballet accessories today—the tutu and the pointe shoes (Laemmli, 2015). While the beautiful and expressive prima ballerinas such as Italian Marie Taglioni, Austrian Fanny Elssler, Italian Carlotta Grisi, and Dane Lucille Grahn (Eliot, 2007) were elevated to almost mythical celebrity status in Romantic-era France, the majority of French women in the Paris Opéra occupied quite different social positions.

The "ballet girls," the *corps de ballet* (who performed in the background of the main *première danseuse*), *figurantes*, and *marcheuses* who had minor roles on stage, entered the dance world through the Opéra school, which was open to all. These girls were often from poor, single-parent families whose mothers simply wanted them to earn at least some salary (Eliot, 2007). Some even performed their roles without any pay in the hope of making it as a dancer. They were relegated to the lowest rank of the dancers and forced to supplement their meager income with prostitution. With the feminization of ballet as a profession, there was an increased male audience for whom the ballet girls personified "unmarried, approachable, erotic beings" (Karthas, 2012, 971).[3] Even the prima ballerinas were assigned private rooms for warm-up (the so-called dancers' corridor), but also for accommodating their lovers.

Towards the end of the nineteenth century, ballet in France was a feminized, eroticized, working-class form of entertainment more frequently performed in music halls than in the Opéra (Karthas, 2012). As a result, "the ballet dancer was no longer a metaphoric symbol of nobility, grace or poetry, but rather conceived first and foremost as a sexual being, a worker, and a titillating subject" (Karthas, 2012, 961).

At the end of the nineteenth century, the epicentre of ballet shifted from France to Imperial Russia where the famous neoclassical ballets such as *Sleeping Beauty*, *Swan Lake*, and *The Nutcracker*, which remain adored archetypes of classical ballet, continued to pay tribute to the Romantic tradition. This was the "golden age of classical ballerinas" (Fisher, 2012, 52), who continued the image of gliding grace and feathery ethereality of the romantic ballet.[4] The ballerina, however, sustained a dual femininity of the natural lightness and grace and the erotic sexuality of a woman's body on public display. In addition, the "exotic" Russian ballet dancers became "all the rage" in world capitals like London (Fisher, 2012, 59). Probably the most famous was Anna Pavlova, who, with her signature piece, *Dying Swan*, is often credited with continuing the traditional, neoclassical heritage of ballet. Pavlova's contemporaries, the Ballets Russes, anticipated the move from the sexualized feminine ballet body to the formalist body of pure movement and to ballet, and dance in general, as an independent art form.

The Ballet Russes' repertoire, which often emphasized the pantomime of (distorted) gestures and postures, moved away from the neoclassical image of the eroticized, fetishized ballerina to shape her into a professional, athletic performer (Karthas, 2012). Although a former member and choreographer of the Ballet Russes, Balanchine had a different vision for his formalist ballets developed particularly in the cultural context of the United States (Morris, 2005). These ballets required a different body shape from the neoclassical or the Ballet Russes ballerinas. Inspired by a range of movement themes, including the classical *danse d'école*, Africanist presence, and surrealism (see Morris, 2005), Balanchine's abstract works, particularly the "leotard ballets" (Kowal, 2014, 78), required a modern "streamlined" and "powerful" ballerina's body (Laemmli, 2015, 3). The Balanchine ballerinas were uniformly trained to expose the lines of their long limbs, lean legs, and extremely thin bodies. They had the simple carriage, strength, speed, clarity, and technical and musical exactness, exemplifying what Morris (2005) defines as an embodiment of "the new power of America" (38). Laemmli (2015) observes that the "Balanchine look" (16) was not only an aesthetic preference, but also a requirement for the extended pointe work. She explains, "The uniqueness of the 'Balanchine body' also depended on particular kinds of novel muscular configurations, configurations that themselves owed much to the pointe shoe: leg muscles that had been shaped to appear unusually lanky, feet that were elongated, enormously flexible, and tapered" (16). Balanchine's formalist interpretation changed the image of the ballerina as naturally expressive, emotional, or openly sexual.

As this volume reveals, popular presentations continue to embrace an image of the long-limbed, thin, and flexible ballerina's body. For example, in Chapter 1 Kate Davies analyzes children's books that picture the ballerina's body, clad in a tutu and pointe shoes, as thin, flexible, and technically proficient. In a very different context, Pirkko Markula and Marianne Clark in Chapter 3 suggest that online barre workouts celebrate the long, thin legs of the formalist ballerina's body shape. Feminist researchers have continued to interrogate the representations of the ideal professional feminine ballet body. Using various theoretical perspectives, these scholars have located the ballet body within the binary of oppression–liberation.

The (Oppressive) Gender Politics of the Feminine Ballet Body

A substantial feminist dance studies scholarship considers the thin, lithe, and hyperflexible ballerina's body oppressive to women (Adair, 1992; Daly, 1987, 1997; Foster, 1996; Novack, 1993). According to these critics, the feminine ballet body maintains traditional gender roles and power arrangements: the ballerinas do whatever it takes (e.g., dieting, extreme training) to obtain the body that has been constructed as the ideal ballet body by artistic directors and choreographers (Adair, 1992; Daly, 1987, 1997; Oliver, 2005). Sherlock (1993) adds that ballerinas' bodies are not just scrutinized by ballet instructors and academy directors, but are also "shaped by wider ideological notions of bodies, movements and good dancing" (39). As a result, the perfect feminine ballet physique becomes a disembodied body whose movements (extensions, weightlessness), roles (fairies and swans), and size (petite) are defined by patriarchal structures. From a feminist psychoanalytic perspective, Foster (1996) demonstrates how the ballerina's body, devoid of power and entirely controlled through the male desire, turns, symbolically, into a phallus to enact male power. Several feminist writers (Adair, 1992, 1993; Albright, 1997; Dempster, 1988; Foster, 1996; Manning, 1997; Wolff, 1997) observe that ballet, similar to film, exposes the female body as an object for the male desiring gaze. According to these researchers, the ballet body is a traditionally feminine body; dominated by patriarchy and sustained by the male gaze, it does not embody potential for women's empowerment.[5]

Ballet scholarship in the late 1990s complicated the disempowering narrative (Aalten, 2004, 2007; Banes, 1998; Fisher, 2012; Foster, 1997). Banes (1998), for example, argues that instead of assuming a positive or negative image, a dialogue that addresses the complex range of ballet representations is needed. Summers-Bremner (2000) further advocates the ballet body as a meeting ground for the masculine and feminine where the female can also have access to male power. These scholars read images, texts, or performance recordings to reveal multiple meanings—some aligning with the traditional femininity, some resisting it—signifying the feminine ballet body. Other feminist researchers have sought to extend the analysis to examine ballet dancers' embodied, lived experiences.

Lived, Embodied Experiences of Disciplinary Ballet

Understanding the "instructional practices and the daily routines that create a dancer's body" (Aalten, 2004, 264) within the

professional world of ballet requires a "more meat and bones approach to the body" (Foster, 1997, 235). Consequently, several ethnographers aim to highlight the lived, bodily experiences of professional
ballet dancers.

The ethnographies conducted within ballet companies (Aalten, 2004, 2007; Wainwright & Turner, 2004, 2006; Wainwright, Williams, & Turner, 2005; Wulff, 1998, 2008) paint a picture of a demanding professional environment where the dancers' bodies are stretched to their limits.[6] Wulff (2008) and Wainwright and Turner (2004, 2006) characterize it as a culture of hardiness that requires the dancers to ignore pain and injuries. The obligatory ideal aesthetics of the ballerina (Aalten, 2004, 2007) requires constant dieting, and according to Aalten (2004, 2007), eating disorders are very common among professional ballerinas. Success in the embodied culture of professional ballet requires both physical capital attained by long, arduous, and disciplinary technical training, and cultural capital—knowledge of the culture of the company as well as the global culture of ballet. This ballet habitus is sustained by a deeply internalized sense of professional discipline obtained from the early days of training (Aalten, 2004, 2007; Wainwright & Turner, 2006) and attachment to one's company (Aalten, 2004, 2007; Wainwright & Turner, 2006). Despite constant pain, frequent injuries, and problems with eating disorders, the ballet dancers sincerely embrace their profession and their identity as dancers.

In addition to professional ballet, several researchers have explored pre-professional or amateur ballet dancers' experiences in training academies, colleges, and universities (Alter, 1997; Bracey, 2004; O'Flynn, Prior, & Gray, 2013; Pickard, 2012, 2013; Wellard, Pickard, & Bailey, 2007). Similar to professional ballet dancers, the pre-professional, young dancers become explicitly aware and accepting of the expectation to comply with the ideal ballet body (Pickard, 2012, 2013; Wellard, Pickard, & Bailey, 2007). Through regular training, dancers pick up the norms and codes of behaviour that they then transfer to their professional careers. However, ballet is also an important means of self-expression and a creative outlet that allows the young dancers to feel "free" (Wellard, Pickard, & Bailey, 2007, 88). In her study of ballet dancers in university and college programs, Alter (1997) reports that participants described dance as satisfying their creative needs and providing an emotional release they did not experience in other areas of their lives. Similarly, O'Flynn, Pryor, and Gray (2013) found that while the young dancers described the pressures associated with achieving the slim, toned, flawless body ideal, they all felt sensual enjoyment of dance that offered an important outlet for expression.

Reflecting on these findings, ballet should not be understood simply as an oppressive practice. There appears to be something salient about the experience of being a dancer and the physical practice of ballet that non-professional dancers enjoy. While the same aesthetic rules of the world of professional ballet are acknowledged by non-professionals, they seem somewhat tempered. However, similar to the research of professional ballet dancers' experiences, the findings align themselves along two main narratives: ballet as a highly disciplinary practice and ballet as a means of self-expression and enjoyment. This line of thought is a helpful place to start further study into the experiences of non-professional dancers to examine more carefully how ballet, and the ballet body, shapes and is shaped by greater social contexts.

These research findings, indeed, prompted several authors in our collection to examine how recreational ballet dancers make sense of their experiences. Marianne Clark examines the lived experiences of teenage ballet dancers who trained seriously in a private studio setting in Chapter 4. While aware of the limiting ideal image of the ballet body and the dangers of disciplinary training, these dancers drew from several other discursive resources available to them to make sense of their experiences. In Chapter 5, Carolyn Millar, inspired by phenomenology, focuses on exposing positive experiences of young ballet dancers who, after completing their studio training or unsuccessfully exploring a professional career, sought to continue in a recreational, contemporary dance setting. These dancers revealed that finding an appropriate technical level of training and social context assisted in a successful transition and provided an avenue for their continued passion for and enjoyment of dance. In a different context, in Chapter 7, Kelsie Acton and Lindsay Eales contemplate what it means to introduce ballet training to their budding professional integrated dancers who requested more exposure to ballet. They debated how to achieve the positive aspects of a higher technical level without the discipline that produces docile dancers.

The Contemporary Ballet Body in Popular and Everyday Contexts

Our book is divided into sections that address, first, representations of ballet in contemporary media, and, second, lived experiences of ballet. We, however, aim to avoid locating the mediated ballet body in opposition to the lived experiences of dancing ballet. While some authors in our book draw from phenomenology (Millar in Chapter 5), we also employ poststructuralist Deleuzian (Chapters 2 and 3) and Foucauldian (Chapters 1, 4, 6, and 7) frameworks to understand the lived ballet body within the power/discourse nexus defining various contemporary contexts for ballet bodies in Canada. In so doing, we do not install the ballet body as a liberating or resistant body, a mediated or lived body, or an exemplary or failed feminist project. Instead, we are interested in illustrating how the feminine ballet body, as historically produced, is now shaped by the current (dominant) ways of knowing dance and how the dancing selves are then formed within these forces. In addition, we are interested in highlighting how the ballet body has moved outside of the professional, high-art context of theatre to assume multiple meanings in various everyday contexts.

To open the first part of the book, Ballet in the Contemporary Media, Davies's chapter, "Reading the Ballet Body in Children's Fiction," examines how popular understandings of the ballet body are constructed through contemporary picture books for children. Her Foucauldian analysis of both the visual and articulable components demonstrates that the dominant understanding of the ballet body as beautiful and disciplined in these children's books informs contemporary notions of gender, active bodies, and physical culture.

In Chapter 2, "*So You Think You Can Dance*: The Feminine Ballet Body in a Popular Reality Show," Markula also turns her attention to the increasing visibility of ballet within popular culture through her analysis of the popular reality dance program, *So You Think You Can Dance* (SYTYCD). Drawing upon the Deleuzian concept of "face," she questions the capacity of the ballet body to disrupt the molar dancing identity through its popularized presentation.

In Chapter 3, "Ballet-Inspired Workouts: Intersections of Ballet and Fitness," Markula and Clark examine how ballet intersects with women's fitness in popular ballet barre-based workouts appearing in women's fitness magazines. Similar to Davies but drawing on the concept of the discursive formation (Deleuze, 1988; Foucault, 1976), Markula and Clark analyze both the visible (images) and articulable (texts) forms of knowledge that appear in the online version of the workouts to understand what type of feminine body these workouts promote in popular fitness media.

In the second part of the collection, Lived Experiences of Ballet in Contemporary Culture, the focus shifts to the lived experiences of those who study, teach, and choreograph ballet in contemporary non-professional settings. In Chapter 4, "Multiple Bodies: In the Studio with Adolescent Ballet Dancers," Clark seeks to understand how adolescent female dancers in recreational studios make meaning of their ballet bodies. Through interviews and fieldwork guided by Foucault's concept of discourse, Clark identifies multiple meanings assigned to ballet bodies that are prompted by the body in motion and extend beyond mere aesthetics.

Like Clark, Millar turns her attention to the recreational dance studio in Chapter 5, "'Moving for Pleasure:' The Positive Experiences of Ballet Dancers Moving into Recreational

Contemporary Dance." Through a phenomenological lens, Millar asks how trained ballet dancers who continue to dance in a recreational environment interpret and understand positive dance experiences. Millar's participants describe negotiating dance experiences throughout their long-time participation and, as a result, complicate understandings of ballet as an oppressive practice.

In Chapter 6, "At the Barre: Ethical Training for Beginner Ballet Class," Vandekerkhove considers the ethical implications of teaching ballet in popular, non-elite settings. Drawing on her personal experience as a ballet teacher and guided by Foucault's concepts of relational power and disciplinary techniques, Vandekerkhove asks in what ways contemporary ballet training is disciplinary and how it might be changed. Her analysis results in recommendations for adapting teaching practices to be more ethical, while negotiating the pragmatics of teaching beginner ballet students.

In Chapter 7, "Ballet for All Bodies? Tensions in Teaching Ballet Technique within an Integrated Dance Context," Acton and Eales focus on explicitly challenging dominant notions of dance and ability. Informed by their personal experience as dancers, choreographers, and performers, Acton and Eales use a conversational format to illustrate how they navigate tensions encountered when teaching ballet within integrated dance. Informed by Foucauldian theory, Laban movement analysis, brain-compatible dance education, traditional ballet technique, and the practices of adaptation and transformation, the authors work to provide dancers with tools and choices about how to train their bodies.

Ballet as an art form and, alongside it, the feminine ballet body, has evolved through the changing political landscapes and has expressed social ideals of its time, but has also elicited social change. Even in the 1700s, Noverre insisted that instead of frivolous diversion and spectacle, ballet was to depict the profoundness of the human condition (Eliot, 2007). Michel Fokine, the pre-eminent ballet master for the Imperial Russian Ballet and later the choreographer for the Ballets Russes, saw ballet as a vehicle for social change (Garafola, 2009). More currently, Forsythe considered ballet as a subjugated knowledge loaded with political potential (Hammond, 2013). At the same time, ballet, patronized by the aristocracy or wealthy balletomanes, represented traditional social values and gender politics. In addition, ballet emerged as a male-dominated institution. Even during the Romantic era, the ballet masters, choreographers, theatre directors, and the audience were male. While possibly enjoying increased female audiences today, ballet continues to be directed by men despite the fact that the majority of the dancers are women. Perhaps as a consequence, ballet has challenged some notions of dominant masculinity through openly homoerotic displays of the male ballet dancer, yet the ballerina's femininity has remained largely unquestioned (Alterowich, 2014).

The image of the ballerina's feminine body is characterized by several binaries. One of the most enduring binaries refers to the nature of ballet itself: Is expressiveness or technical virtuosity essential for ballet as a dance form? The shifting emphasis between the ballerina's emotional expression and technical virtuosity embedded another binary: the female body constructed as ethereal and innocent versus the sexual and material ballet body. Several feminist dance researchers further located the ballerina with the binary of oppression and liberation. We hope that our collection will prompt further dialogue about how these binaries that have historically seen in dance research and ballet practice might be dissolved or disrupted to allow for more complex understandings of ballet and the ballet body.

Notes

1. The Ballets Russes (1909–1929) has evoked significant scholarly interest (Acocella, 1984; Garafola, 2009; Homans, 2010; Järvinen, 2014; Sgourev, 2015), possibly because of its generally acknowledged transformative impact on ballet. Some scholars note that the Ballets Russes saved ballet from inevitable decline, and many credit its success to its formidable leader, Sergei Diaghilev, a Russian aristocrat with good connections to the art world (Eliot, 2007; Järvinen, 2014; Sgourev, 2015). Diaghilev was able to combine the work of budding modernist composers, artists, authors, and dancers into sumptuous

and stunning ballet performances that catered to multiple audiences (the high society, the wealthy Franco-Judeans, the demi-monde, the avant garde artists, the Russian emigrées) of wealth or intellectuality, particularly in France (Järvinen, 2014; Sgourev, 2015).

2. See also Morris's (1996) Butlerian analysis of *The Hard Nut* as a subversion of gender roles.

3. For the condition of the "ballet girls" in Victorian England, see Carter (2005).

4. In her account of Tamara Karsavina's career, Eliot (2007) describes ballet training at the Imperial Ballet School in St. Petersburg, Russia, where ballet was directly under the jurisdiction of the Imperial Court. This meant secure support from the tsar's "own purse" (70), but also loyalty to the monarch. Unlike in France, the students were carefully selected for long and slowly progressing training in an exam that also included tests in writing, mathematics, and musical scales; thus, the students did not come from the lowest, uneducated classes. Once at school, the students lived a life isolated from "real" life and were carefully supervised by the matrons. There were, nevertheless, rumours of Russian ballerinas becoming mistresses of the Romanoffs or other wealthy ballet patrons (Eliot, 2007; Fisher, 2012).

5. Instead of the physical prowess in ballet, several critical feminist scholars (Adair, 1992; Albright, 1997; Daly, 1992, 1997; Foster, 1986; Novack, 1990; Thomas, 1996; Wolff, 1997) offered modern dance, postmodern dance, or contact improvisation as alternative liberating body practices. Wolff (1997), for example, divides dance into ballet, modern dance, and postmodern dance to illustrate this point. Modern dance, originally created by women dancers as a reaction to ballet, could potentially act as a liberating body practice but tends to locate the body within codified technical training systems and masks femininity behind the patriarchal premise of a natural body. Postmodern dance draws attention to the body itself, and thus provides the highest potential for liberating dance practice that uses the body in a truly political way. While the three-tiered hierarchy—ballet, modern dance, postmodern dance—is critiqued as too dogmatic, problematic, and wrought with definitional problems, it seems to persist within the scholarly dance studies literature despite the blurring boundaries of dance forms.

6. Aalten (2004) studied several ballet companies in the Netherlands. Wainwright, Williams, and Turner (2005; Wainwright & Turner, 2006, 238) conducted an ethnography of the Royal Ballet in London, UK, and Wulff's ethnography (1998, 2008) examined ballet as global culture and focused on several ballet companies: the Royal Swedish Ballet in Stockholm, the Royal Ballet in London, the American Ballet Theatre in New York, and Ballett Frankfurt in Frankfurt-am-Main.

References

Aalten, A. (2004). "The moment when it all comes together": Embodied experiences in ballet. *European Journal of Women's Studies, 11*(3), 263–76. doi:10.1177/1350506804044462

Aalten, A. (2007). Listening to the dancer's body. *The Sociological Review, 55*(Supp. 1), 109–25.

Acocella, J. R. (1984). *The reception of Diaghilev's Ballets Russes by artists and intellectuals in Paris and London, 1909–1914* (Unpublished doctoral dissertation). Rutgers University, NJ.

Adair, C. (1992). *Women and dance: Sylphs and sirens.* London: MacMillan.

Adair, C. (1993). Viewing women: The display of the female body in dance. In C. Brackenridge (Ed.), *Body matters: Leisure images and lifestyles* (39–44). Eastborne, UK: Leisure Studies Association.

Albright, A. C. (1997). *Choreographing difference: The body and identity in contemporary dance.* Hanover, NH: Wesleyan University Press.

Alter, J. (1997). Why dance students pursue dance: Studies of dance students from 1953 to 1993. *Dance Research Journal, 29,* 70–89.

Alterowitz, G. (2014). Embodying a queer worldview: The contemporary ballets of Katy Pyle and Deborah Lohse. *Dance Chronicle, 37*(3), 335–66. doi:10.1080/01472526.2014.957599

Banes, S. (1998). *Dancing women: Female bodies on stage.* London: Routledge.

Bracey, L. (2004). Voicing connections: An interpretive study of university dancers' experiences. *Research in Dance Education, 5,* 7–24.

Briginshaw, V. A. (2001). Architectural spaces in the choreography of William Forsythe and De Keersmaeker's Rosas Danst Rosas. In V. A. Briginshaw (Ed.), *Dance, space and subjectivity* (183–206). Basingstoke, UK: Palgrave.

Boyd, J. (2004). Dance, culture, and popular film. *Feminist Media Studies, 4*(1), 67–83.

Carter, A. (2005). *Dance and dancers in the Victorian and Edwardian music hall ballet.* Hampshire and Burlington, UK: Ashgate.

Daly, A. (1987). The Balanchine woman: Of hummingbirds and channel swimmers. *The Drama Review, 31,* 8–21.

Daly, A. (1992). Dance history and feminist theory: Reconsidering Isadora Duncan and the male gaze. In L. Senelick (Ed.), *Gender and performance: The presentation of difference in the performing arts* (239–59). Hanover, NH: University Press of New England.

Daly, A. (1997). Classical ballet: A discourse of difference. In J. C. Desmond (Ed.), *Meaning in motion: New cultural studies of dance* (111–21). Durham, NC: Duke University Press.

Deleuze, G. (1988). *Foucault.* (S. Hand, Trans.). London: Athlone.

Dempster, E. (1988). Women writing the body: Let's watch a little how she dances. In S. Sheridan (Ed.), *Grafts: Feminist cultural criticism* (35–54). London: Verso.

Eliot, K. (2007). *Dancing lives: Five female dancers from the Ballet d'Action to Merce Cunningham.* Champaign: University of Illinois Press.

Fisher, J. (2012). The Swan brand: Reframing the legacy of Anna Pavlova. *Dance Research Journal, 44*(1), 51–67.

Foster, S. L. (1986). *Reading dancing: Bodies and subjects in contemporary American dance.* Berkeley: University of California Press.

Foster, S. L. (1996). The ballerina's phallic pointe. In S. L. Foster (Ed.), *Corporealities: Dancing, knowledge, culture and power* (1–24). London: Routledge.

Foster, S. L. (1997). Dancing bodies. In J. C. Desmond (Ed.), *Meaning in motion: New cultural studies of dance* (235–58). Durham, NC: Duke University Press.

Foucault, M. (1976). *The archaeology of knowledge and the discourse on language.* (A.M. Sheridan Smith, Trans.). New York: Pantheon Books.

Franko, M. (2011a). Splintered encounters: The critical reception to William Forsythe in the United States, 1979–1989. In S. Spier (Ed.), *William Forsythe and the practice of choreography: It starts from any point* (38–50). New York: Routledge.

Franko, M. (2011b). Archaeological choreographic practices: Foucault and Forsythe. *History of the Humanities, 24*(4), 97–112.

Garafola, L. (2009). *Diaghilev's Ballets Russes.* New York: Da Capo.

Hammond, H. (2013). Dancing against history: (The Royal) Ballet, Forsythe, Foucault, Brecht, and the BBC. *Dance Research, 31*(2), 120–43.

Harris, A. (2007). Choreographing America: Redefining American ballet in the age of consensus. In W. W. Demastes & I. Smith Fischer (Eds.), *Interrogating America through theatre and performance* (139–56). New York: Palgrave MacMillan.

Homans, J. (2010). *Apollo's angels: A history to ballet.* New York: Random House.

Järvinen, H. (2014). Comedy ballet as social commentary: Till Eulenspiegel (1916). *Dance Research, 32*(2), 144–84.

Karthas, I. (2012). The politics of gender and the revival of ballet in early twentieth century France. *Journal of Social History, 45*(3), 960–69.

Kowal, R. J. (2014). "Indian ballerinas toe up": Maria Tallchief and making ballet "American" in the tribal termination era. *Dance Research Journal, 46*(2), 73–96.

Laemmli, W. (2015). A case in pointe: Romance and regimentation at the New York City Ballet. *Technology and Culture, 56*(1), 1–27.

Manning, S. (1997). The female dancer and the male gaze: Feminist critiques of early modern dance. In J. C. Desmond (Ed.), *Meaning in motion: New cultural studies of dance* (153–66). Durham, NC: Duke University Press.

Morris, G. (1996). "Styles of flesh": Gender in the dances of Mark Morris. In G. Morris (Ed.), *Moving words: Re-writing dance* (141–58). New York: Routledge.

Morris, G. (2005). Balanchine's bodies. *Body & Society, 11*, 19–44.

Novack, C. (1990). *Sharing the dance: Contact improvisation and American culture.* Madison: University of Wisconsin Press.

Novack, C. (1993). Ballet, gender and cultural power. In H. Thomas (Ed.), *Dance, gender and power* (34–49). London: MacMillan.

O'Flynn, G., Pryor, Z., & Gray, T. (2013). Embodied subjectivities: Nine young women talking dance. *Journal of Dance Education, 13*(4), 130–38.

Oliver, W. (2005). Reading the ballerina's body: Susan Bordo sheds light on Anastasia Volochkova and Heidi Guenther. *Dance Research Journal, 37*, 38–54.

Pickard, A. (2012). Schooling the dancer: The evolution of an identity as a ballet dancer. *Research in Dance Education, 13*, 25–46.

Pickard, A. (2013). Ballet body belief: Perceptions of an ideal ballet body from young ballet dancers. *Research in Dance Education, 14*, 3–19.

Sgourev, S. V. (2015). Brokerage as catalysis: How Diaghilev's *Ballets Russes* escalated modernism. *Organization Studies, 36*(3), 343–61.

Sherlock, J. (1993). Dance and the culture of the body. In S. Scott & D. Morgan (Eds.), *Body matters: Essays on the sociology of the body* (35–46). Bristol, PA: Taylor & Francis.

Solutions Research Group. (2014, June 10). Massive competition in pursuit of the $5.7 billion Canadian youth sports market. Retrieved from http://www.srgnet.com/2014/06/10/massive-competition-in-pursuit-of-the-5-7-billion-canadian-youth-sports-market/

Summers-Bremner, E. (2000). Reading Irigaray, dancing. *Hypatia, 15*(1), 90–124.

Thomas, H. (1996). Do you want to join the dance? Postmodernism/poststructuralism, the body, and dance. In G. Morris (Ed.), *Moving words: Re-writing dance* (63–87). London: Routledge.

Wainwright, S. P., & Turner, B. S. (2004). Epiphanies of embodiment: Injury, identity and the balletic body. *Qualitative Research, 4*(3), 311–37.

Wainwright, S. P., & Turner, B. S. (2006). Varieties of habitus and the embodiment of ballet. *Qualitative Research, 6*(4), 535–58.

Wainwright, S. P., Williams, C., & Turner, B. S. (2005). Fractured identities: Injury and the balletic body. *Health: An Interdisciplinary Journal for the Social Study of Health, Illness and Medicine, 9*(1), 49–66.

Wellard, I., Pickard, A., & Bailey, R. (2007). "A shock of electricity just sort of goes through my body": Physical activity and embodied reflexive practices in young female ballet dancers. *Gender and Education, 19*(1), 79–91.

Wolff, J. (1997). Re-instating corporeality: Feminism and body politics. In J. C. Desmond (Ed.), *Meaning in motion: New cultural studies of dance* (81–100). Durham, NC: Duke University Press.

Wulff, H. (1998). *Ballet across borders: Career and culture in the world of dancers.* Oxford, UK: Berg.

Wulff, H. (2008). Ethereal expression: Paradoxes of ballet as a global physical culture. *Ethnography, 9*(4), 518–35. doi:10.1177/1466138108096990

I

Ballet in the Contemporary Media

1

READING THE BALLET BODY IN CHILDREN'S FICTION

Kate Z. Davies

The ballerina is an enduring symbol of girlhood (Turk, 2014). As a testament to its popularity, many Canadian girls and women have taken ballet class, owned a pair of ballet slippers, and worn a leotard with a tutu at some point in their lives (Miskec, 2014). Ballet is also visible in mainstream media. For example, *Angelina Ballerina*, a dancing mouse, is a popular computer game, television, and book series read by many girls (Turk, 2014). A number of other children's books have an underlying theme of ballet. These mediated texts, in their part, shape how children come to understand dance and the dancing body, particularly the ballet body, in contemporary society.

To understand what it means to be a dancing body during childhood requires knowledge of how such meanings are produced and reproduced. To achieve this end, I examine the meaning of ballet in children's picture books. This chapter is part of my doctoral research, which analyzes how meanings of the active body are (re)produced across thirty children's picture books. In this discussion, however, I examine six stories about ballet from my larger sample of books about children's physical activity: *Ballerina Rosie,*

Tallulah's Tutu, Ballet Stars, Miss Lina's Ballerinas and the Prince, Ella Bella Ballerina and Swan Lake, and *The Only Boy in Ballet Class.* To begin, I situate the research within the wider body of literature on ballet and children. I then introduce my Foucauldian approach to explain how I conduct my analysis. After presenting my results, I conclude with a discussion of the knowledges that (re)produce the ballet body in children's books. In the review of literature that follows, I critique how gender has been analyzed in the academic literature on children's active bodies, thereby providing a rationale for the Foucauldian-inspired approach underpinning this study.

Appropriate Gendered Identities?

Children's literature is a powerful medium through which meanings of the body are normalized and conveyed during childhood (Hunt, 1985; Rogers, 2008; Saric, 2005; Stallcup, 2004). Paterson and Lach (1990) argue that "books can and do have profound effects on children" (195). Moreover, Worland (2008) asserts that

> picture books exert a unique influence on their audience...Most significantly, the audience receives messages in the text at a point in their lives when they are especially impressionable and when they first begin to formulate ideas about culture, society and values...In addition, picture books...promote ideas with increased impact because of the power of the illustrations...Thus, picture books deliver their messages twice, with words and illustrations... Research shows that children translate the values and messages in books into attitudes and behavior...Their behavior and their expectations of other's behaviors often reveal acceptance and conformity to what they have been most exposed to in books. (42–43)

Although scholarship that examines representations of children's active bodies is scarce, there is some research regarding gender roles in children's literature. These studies focus on the body as a site where meanings of disability, race, ethnicity, and gender are (re)produced and/or contested (Hamilton, Anderson, Broaddus, & Young, 2006; Hunter, 1982; Matthews, 2009; Nilges & Spencer, 2002; Rogers & Christian, 2007; Singleton, 2004; Stott, 1979; Weiller & Higgs, 1989).

For example, in a study that analyzes a project developed to make children's bodies with disabilities visible in children's picture books, Matthews (2009) found that the visibility of these bodies was contingent upon and constrained by dominant social understandings of disability that tended to render disabled bodies "impermissible." Hamdi and Newbery (2004) further observe that children's books are generally devoid of discussions of impermissible bodies. Such deliberate omissions are linked to the belief that inappropriate references to the body may encourage children's "uncivilized behavior" (Stallcup, 2004, 91). Given that ballet is considered to require highly able bodies, I am also interested in how impermissible bodies are reproduced in these books.

Rogers and Christian (2007) examine the construction of race in a selection of multicultural children's books that, as they argue, "intentionally bring Whiteness to the surface" (21). Their intent was to reveal how children's literature marginalizes people of colour. Based on their findings, the authors suggest that multiple and contradictory meanings underpin the messages conveyed in the selected books. For example, they note that "the talk in texts between White characters sometimes re-centers Whiteness and other times disrupts Whiteness as the center" (21). While the multicultural children's literature aims to address the oppression of marginalized populations, based on Rogers and Christian's (2007) study, there is also potential to perpetuate oppression by revealing "the effects, both productive (when Whiteness is decentered) and repressive (when Whiteness is re-centered), of discourse and through them, the use of power" (47). I am interested in examining how children's ballet books might represent race and ethnicity considering that high-art "theatre dance," such as ballet, with studio fees, has often been seen, at least in Canada, as a middle-class, white women's and girls' activity (Boyd, 2004).

Relevant to my topic of the depictions of the ballet body, several studies have focused on the gender differences in children's books. In a study of the pictorial representation of gender and physical activity level in Caldecott Medal–winning children's literature between 1940 and 1999, Nilges and Spencer (2002) found that both females and physical activity were underrepresented in these awarding-winning books. In a survey of two hundred popular children's books, Hamilton et al. (2006) concluded that female characters continued to be underrepresented. In addition, while twice as many male characters occupied jobs outside the home, nurturing behaviour appeared to be more common among female characters despite the decline of such behaviours from 1970 to 1980. Although female characters (79%) were just as likely as male characters (86%) to be portrayed as active bodies, the study did not specify whether the types of activities girls and boys engaged in were similar (Hamilton et al., 2006, 762). However, according to Weiller and Higgs (1989), "many reading materials available in the school libraries present certain prescribed roles for girls and boys in sport activities" (66). For example, "in dance and tennis females were represented six out of six times [and]…five out of six times in gymnastics as opposed to three out of six by males" (Weiller & Higgs, 1989, 66). Based on their findings, Weiller and Higgs (1989) conclude that these readings reified the traditional gender order. As I noted at the beginning of my chapter, ballet tends to be popular particularly among girls. Thus, part of my concern in this chapter is whether ballet picture books provide a different gender balance.

Some researchers have, indeed, focused on books aimed specifically at girls. For example, Dohnt and Tiggemann (2008) conducted a study "to evaluate the potential for the picture book, *Shapesville*, to promote positive body image in young girls" (222). The story, which depicts five friends who range in shape, size, and colour, is intended to encourage diversity and acceptance. Based on their results, Dohnt and Tiggemann (2008) conclude that "*Shapesville* can be a successful prevention tool for use with young girls" (232). For example, the study reports, "[The girls'] knowledge of the five food groups increased significantly [after reading *Shapesville*]. The promotion of healthy eating is important to obesity prevention and *Shapesville* may assist in this cause" (231). Dohnt and Tiggemann (2008) then state, "The girls reported learning that appearance is not important, commonly, *'It doesn't matter what you look like'*" (231). The authors conclude that *Shapesville* appears to be a useful tool in the prevention of obesity and disordered eating. In a study of images featuring Barbie and the Emme doll (the latter based on a plus-size model), Dittmar, Halliwell, and Ive (2006) suggest that by the age of eight, girls who had been exposed to thin-ideal body images may internalize these images to the point where viewing images of a larger body, such as the Emme doll, actually elicits a negative response toward the larger size image.

Instead of body image concerns, Kane (1998) examines the portrayal of female protagonists in sport novels published between 1970 and 1997. Based on earlier work, she organized and analyzed the texts according to one of two themes: "lone girl" and "women's team sport" (236). Using a feminist perspective, she found "strong support for heterosexual relationships" across the novels (256). According to Kane, this "redirection" is problematic for two reasons. First, it "undermines women's connections with each other." Second, "it simultaneously reassures the reader that all of the female characters are unequivocally heterosexual" (256). Through her analysis, Kane also demonstrates that to be accepted as an athlete, female protagonists must behave just as their male counterparts would, notably when injured. Singleton's (2004) analysis of female protagonists from two early twentieth-century adventure series for teenage girls supported this latter finding. Like Kane (1998), she employs a feminist perspective to find that "these highly active and physically competent female characters support, through their continuous iterations of femininity, the ideological attribution of maleness to physical skill, risk taking and adventures" (Singleton, 2004, 131). These findings provide interesting intersections with my research on ballet where the injury rates, similar to sport, are high. However, it must be noted that the sport research focused on young adult sports fiction or women's sports fiction. Indeed, research on the impact of ballet in children's developing bodies exists.

A significant portion of the academic literature investigating the influence of ballet on children is concerned with the physiological (Kadel, Donaldson-Fletcher, Gerberg, & Micheli, 2005; Moller & Masharawi, 2011; Stokić, Srdić, & Barak, 2005) or psychosocial (Bettle, Bettle, Neumarker, & Neumarker, 2001) effects of ballet training. Moller and Masharawi (2011), for example, examine the effect of participating in ballet on the developing child's posture. They found that young children who engaged in ballet training to increase flexibility were predisposed to back problems later in life. With the exception of Pickard (2013), who, drawing from Bourdieu, examines "what is perceived and believed to be an ideal ballet body by young ballet dancers" (3), research that critiques what it means to be a dancing body is limited to adolescent and adult dancers, similar to sport research (Oliver, 2005; Sherlock, 1991; Wainwright, Williams, & Turner, 2007). Moreover, most of the dance studies research focuses on the ideal body of the female ballerina.

Although research on girls' sporting or physically active bodies is rare, the two studies I identified to examine ballet in children's literature focus specifically on girls. In her essay about the prominence of the foot in children's stories about ballet, Miskec (2014) suggests that "ballet is the perfect space for ideal femininity: thin bodies, frilly skirts, speechlessness; graceful movements making it all look easy while hiding the pain, physical anguish for beauty" (240). In particular, Miskec argues that the image of the ballet foot is problematic not only because it sexualizes young girls, but also because it simultaneously infantilizes the female dancers whom these girls epitomize. In contrast, Turk (2014), who studies American children's literature and girls, contends that images of ballet, specifically "literary representations of ballet in girls' culture...can be used to speak to contemporary girls' lives and imaginations, including ways in which ballet provides enriching girlhood experience" (483). For example, she discusses how the princess image of the ballerina provides space for Olivia, the dancing pig, to shed the stereotypical Disney princess/ballerina costume for ones that represent princesses of different cultures such as India. Turk challenges Miskec, asserting, "'ideal femininity'...can engage young people in valuable questions about the art form's past, present, and future" (501). Although relevant and necessary, these two studies do not employ a systematic social science methodology to evidence either one of their arguments.

Based on the reading of previous literature, a certain type of "ideal femininity" (thin, pale skin, heterosexual, engaged in nurturing activities but enduring pain) appears to persist in children's books across several physical activity contexts. These studies use a variety of theoretical and methodological approaches. I aim to continue to examine the representations of the ballet body in children's picture books, but employ a Foucauldian theoretical approach to guide my analysis. This approach not only highlights what type of body is represented but also examines why certain representations persist in these books.

Foucauldian Approach to Children's Active Bodies

To examine how children's bodies are (re)produced in children's picture books with the unifying theme of ballet, I draw from Michel Foucault's ideas about power, knowledge, and the body. More specifically, I consider how ballet functions as a truth game that shapes meanings of the dancing body through children's picture books.

Foucault (1980) was interested in the relationship between power/knowledge and what he termed "discourse," or the ways that we know about a topic or phenomenon, such as ballet. Some discourses, he noted, become dominant over time, in a discontinuous manner, thereby making it difficult to trace a particular discourse back to a particular individual or instance (Markula & Pringle, 2006). Moreover, Foucault asserted that discourses are constrained and enabled by the knowledge available at a given time and within a given context. Therefore, of the discourses that are available or possible, only a few are actually reproduced (Markula & Pringle, 2006). For example, based on my literature review, a certain way of understanding femininity was reproduced in children's books. These dominant discourses do not represent truth per se, but instead operate as "truthful," what Foucault (1980) refers to as "effects of truth" (94) that then circulate through texts such as children's books.

Dominant discourses are those that have endured a process of division and rejection whereby competing discourses are discarded, not because these discourses are less "true," but because dominant discourses sustain the power-relation of the specific sociohistoric context in which they operate (Markula & Pringle, 2006). It was the process of how a particular discourse becomes dominant and produces a truth-effect that interested Foucault and underpinned his approach to discourse analysis (Markula & Silk, 2011). I discuss this approach in more detail, in the Methods section. For the purpose of this discussion, it is necessary to explain Foucault's understanding of discourse in terms of its relation to power/knowledge.

Central to Foucault's theorization of power as relational is the understanding that power operates through discourse to legitimate certain forms of knowledge and not others. More specifically, Foucault (1972) asserts, "The exercise of power perpetually creates knowledge and, conversely, knowledge constantly induces effects of power...It is not possible for power to be exercised without knowledge, [sic] it is impossible for knowledge not to engender power" (52). He was particularly interested in how the effects of power/knowledge operate to produce subjects. Foucault argued that, like "truth," the self is discursively produced and is able to change over time. According to Markula and Pringle (2006), "Foucault's theory of discourse acts to decenter the significance of individual humans and consciousness" (30).[1]

Foucault (1972) uses the analogy of an archaeological dig to explain the process he employed to uncover how power is linked to knowledge through discourse. The purpose of this process was not to prove a particular truth, but instead to understand how some discourses become reified while others are rejected (Markula & Pringle, 2006). In this chapter, I theorize how power/knowledge operate to produce truth-effects in children's stories about ballet. More specifically, I employ Foucault's understanding of truth-effect to analyze how these ballet books function as a site where meanings of the dancing body are (re)produced. I consider how the discourses and practices represented in six stories produce understandings of the dancing body by normalizing certain types of dancing bodies as legitimate and not others. I then consider how these understandings are connected to power relations of wider society. I, therefore, draw from Foucault's concepts of power/knowledge and discourse to ask, what does it mean to be a ballet body? And how is the ballet body normalized within the context of particular stories? These questions not only inform the theoretical underpinnings of this research, but also the choice of methods, which I now address.

Methods

Methodological concerns informed the choice of medium (picture books) and the types of texts analyzed (written and visual). In my original research, I employed "criterion sampling" that included thirty books, of which six focused exclusively on ballet (Markula & Silk, 2011, p.115). I then employed Foucauldian discourse analysis "to analyze the ways knowledge is connected to power by focusing on texts" (Markula & Silk, 2011, p.129).

Because picture books include both written and visual texts, I included both in my analysis. During the first step, the "analysis of articulable texts," I identified concepts and individual statements (Markula & Silk, 2011, 131). I then linked the individual statements to general domains of discourse. Foucault (1972) indicates that discourse is sometimes treated as "an individualizable group of statements, and sometimes as a regulated practice that accounts for a certain number of statements" (80). Therefore, within the context of this chapter, "general domains of all statements" refer to the scientific knowledges, such as aesthetics, whereas "individual statements" refer to dance.

Although Foucault (1972) did not apply his analytical techniques to visual texts, his conceptualization of how power/knowledge operates to discipline the body informed this type of analysis. Therefore, during the second step, analysis of visual texts, I looked for instances in which disciplinary power was invested in the body through disciplinary techniques (space, time, movement/ exercise, and composition of forces) (Foucault, 1977) to produce "docile bodies," bodies that had internalized this power and, as a result, became more productive bodies (138). For example, I analyzed how the four characteristics of space (enclosure, partitioning, functionality, and organization of bodies in space) were used in the illustrations to discipline the body, thereby normalizing a certain type of body as acceptable and appropriate. Because I was interested in the representation of the active body, I added a fifth technique, which I labelled bodily appearance.

Analysis

Due to the scope of this chapter, I will discuss three themes I identified through the analysis of written texts: (1) ballet is practiced primarily by girls; (2) accomplished ballerinas wear beautiful tutus and pointe shoes; and (3) the lone dancer is male. I address each theme separately, weaving the analysis together with the visual texts. At times, the discussion of visual analysis appears to dominate that of the written text. There are two explanations for this. First, because I analyzed picture books, the ratio of visual to written text is approximately two-thirds visual to one-third written. Second, due to copyright laws, it was too complicated to include illustrations. Thus, a more lengthy explanation of the visuals was required to support the analysis.

Ballet Is Practiced Primarily by Girls

Across the texts, the dancing body was portrayed in a variety of spaces, both indoors and out. The dance studio was the most common space, featured in five of the six books (Ferguson & Goode, 2012; Gruska & Wummer, 2007; Holub & McNicholas, 2012; Maccarone & Davenier, 2011; Singer & Boiger, 2011). Because most of the dancers in these books were girls taught by women, the ballet space (the studio) conveyed a uniform understanding of the ballet girls' bodies and of ballet as a female activity. This finding supports Weiller and Higgs's (1989) claim that girls tend to be portrayed engaging in gendered activities such as dance and gymnastics, while boys tend to be underrepresented in such activities.

Both the text and the visuals supported a similar reading of the gendered ballet body: female protagonists were generally portrayed with skinny arms, skinny legs, and a slightly protruding tummy. With one exception (Singer & Boiger, 2011), male protagonists were portrayed with slim arms, slim legs, and flat tummies. The contrast between the shape and size of the lone male dancer with that of female dancers reifies the masculine ideal of the male ballet body as stronger and more athletic than the flexible, graceful, and perfect female ballet body (Adams, 2005). In addition, such images sustain the belief that active bodies are thin, healthy bodies (Hemming, 2007).

Most stories included one male character in addition to one or two female background characters of different ethnic and racial origins. In contrast to fair-skinned dancers, those with dark skin were depicted as either shorter or taller than the protagonist and more rotund, or less proficient, than other dancers (Ferguson & Goode, 2012; Singer & Boiger, 2011). These findings demonstrate that children of different racial and ethic backgrounds continue to be marginalized in children's literature (Boyd, 2004; Rogers & Christian, 2007). Characters with a disability were absent in all of the books, thereby normalizing the able body as the ideal dancing body. Thus, similar to Matthews (2009), who asserts that children with a disability tend to be excluded from children's books, dancers who require wheelchairs or walking sticks, who are overweight, or who could otherwise be classified as "unhealthy" are not visible in these stories.

Foucault (1977) refers to the specific use of space to contain, organize, individualize, and regulate the body as "the arts of distribution" (141). Although the studios in the books are enclosed spaces, the layouts are open (either square or rectangular in shape) with ballet barres lining up to four walls depending on the size and placement of windows. Dancers often occupy space at the barre, in linear formation, with the instructor watching from the centre of the room. From this central location, the instructor is able to observe each dancer in an effective and efficient manner. In addition, when each dancer occupies their designated space, their positions at the barre serve as "functional sites" for the instructor to observe and correct individual performances of specialized movements (Foucault, 1977, 143). For example, in *Ballet Stars*, when one ballerina asserts, "The music starts, we take our places" (Holub & McNicholas, 2012, 16), the visuals portray a row of three little dancers standing at the barre, each striking a different pose.

Foucault (1977) notes that "what is specific to the disciplinary penalty is non-observance, that which does not measure up to the rule, that which departs from it" (178). Errors such as loss of balance due to poor posture or positioning cause a dancer to spill out of the small, designated space, disrupting those in close proximity. For example, in *Ballerina Rosie*, when Rosie loses her balance, she is reprimanded: "Crash. Rosie's foot was twisted and she tripped into Francesca. 'Rosie Red Curls, point your feet!'" (Ferguson & Goode, 2012, 15). Such disruptions draw attention to the little dancer, rendering her body visible in a manner that is uncomfortable and encourages her to concentrate and work harder to avoid being the object of both the instructor's and the other dancers' gaze. Normalizing judgement, which makes bodies compliant through a process of individuation and differentiation, functions to correct Rosie's body as the comments made her aware that the teacher, and possibly the other dancers, observed her stumble.

Large mirrors adorn the wall behind as well as those opposite the ballet barre, providing multiple angles from which to view the dancers' movements. For example, in *Tallulah's Tutu*, the teacher emphasizes the importance of correcting the body by using the mirror: "Tallulah, look in the mirror. Can you make your back straighter?" (Singer & Boiger, 2011, 13). In this example, the mirrors amplify the teacher's gaze. The teacher is able to survey her students' bodies through the mirror without actually looking at the dancer. In addition, the mirrors function as disciplinary mechanisms that direct the individual's gaze back upon the self. For example, in *Ballerina Rosie*, upon observing her reflection in the mirror, the protagonist attempts to correct her posture: "Rosie pushed her shoulders back and held her head high, but in the long dance mirror, she looked like a wilted flower" (Ferguson & Goode, 2012, 14). The capacity to correct one's own behaviour, or body position, without recourse from the teacher, suggests, as Foucault (1977) might argue, that Rosie has internalized the teacher's gaze. Foucault might conceptualize a body, such as Rosie, that self-corrects based on the teacher's advice in order to achieve perfect body positioning and timing everywhere, a "docile body" (138). For example, Rosie corrects her posture while at school, away from the watchful eye of her dance instructor: "During school on Monday Rosie made sure she had perfect posture, just like the prima ballerinas. She took small ladylike steps everywhere she went. She crossed her legs daintily when she sat in the lunchroom" (Ferguson & Goode, 2012, 17). The scene described above exemplifies the effect of disciplinary power on the dancing body. Subject to the teacher's gaze, Rosie's body is transformed and improved from wilted flower to elegant young girl. Foucault (1977) might argue that docility produces proficient and skilled ballerinas: perfect ballerinas. He states that "a body is docile that may be subjected, used, transformed and improved" (136).

Accomplished Ballerinas Wear Beautiful Tutus and Pointe Shoes

Based on my analysis, the unifying idea that "practice makes perfect and perfect is beautiful" normalizes understandings of the dancing body. For example, in *Ballerina Rosie*, the dance instructor asserts, "Today ladies we will work on your foot positions. First, second, third" (Ferguson & Goode, 2012, 19). This quotation exemplifies the idea that ballet is about practicing specialized footwork. If Rosie hopes to be recognized as a successful dancer, she has to master these positions. Likewise, the dancers in *Ballet Stars* practice specialized movements: "Ballet arms, ballet feet, toes point out and fingers meet" (Holub & McNicholas, 2012, 8–10). In *Tallulah's Tutu*, the reader learns that "Tallulah practiced everyday" (Singer & Boiger, 2011, 1), while in *Ballerina Rosie*, "Every morning before breakfast, Rosie would practice with bear" (Ferguson & Goode, 2012, 2). Finally, in *Ella Bella Ballerina and Swan Lake*, the dance teacher, Madame Rosa, reminds Ella Bella to practice at home: "Now good night my little swan-girl...don't forget to practice your dancing" (Mayhew, 2011, 27). Both the written and visual texts normalize understandings of the ballet body as one that moves perfectly, which is achieved through practice.

Practice is not restricted to female dancers. Both male and female dancing bodies are portrayed engaging in the repetition required to become accomplished dancers. For example, in *The Only Boy in Ballet Class*, Tucker practices at home every morning while he waits for ballet class to begin: "First he has to leap...then he has to spin...after that he has to go way up on tiptoe" (Gruska & Wummer, 2007, 2). Foucault (1977) asserts, "Disciplinary punishment is, in the main, isomorphic with obligation itself; it is not so much the vengeance of an outraged law as its repetition, reduplicated insistence" (180). Thus, ballet dancers do not seem to think repetitive exercise is punishment but rather a necessary and even enjoyable part of becoming a dancer, as indicated by Tallulah, Rosie, and Tucker's commitment to practice outside the dance studio.

Although male and female dancing bodies are linked to the perfection of movements, similar to the literature on children's sport (Drummond, 2003; Garrett, 2004), the similarity ends here. In my sample of children's books, female dancers' beauty is at times the outcome of perfect positioning and posture. For example, "[Tallulah] can you make your back straighter?" (Singer & Boiger, 2011, 11). At other times, instead of being graceful, perfect movement is achieved by wearing the appropriate accessories. For example, in *Ballerina Rosie*, Rosie performs beautifully when she wears her red satin pointe shoes: "In class in her new shoes, Rosie did a perfect plié and a graceful arabesque, and she was the best in the class at the pirouette" (Ferguson & Goode, 2012, 23–24).

As I noted previously, in the texts I analyzed, docility produces perfection and perfection is associated with beautiful ballerinas. Both the written and visual texts suggest that ballerinas who work hard to achieve perfection, who became docile bodies, are rewarded with beautiful accessories such as tutus and pointe shoes. For example, the female dancers in *Ballet Stars* are rewarded with new costumes for their dance recital: "Ballet show today, hooray! We all dress up in a fancy way. Sparkly ribbons. Ballet shoes. Bright white tights and new tutus" (Holub & McNicholas, 2012, 4–7). Although there was one male dancer in this troupe, no reference is made to what he will wear during the recital.

For the female dancing body, perfection and beauty are closely connected with the quality of the movements performed and the types of accessories accomplished ballerinas wore, such as tutus and pointe shoes. Beautiful tutus and pointe shoes, therefore, make visible the accomplishments of the wearer. In contrast, the dancers, who wear plain bodysuits and ballet slippers, are visible for their lack of perfection. For example, in *Tallulah's Tutu*, the protagonist asserts, "I am a very, very good dancer...and I will get my tutu someday. And she did" (Singer & Boiger, 2012, 28–29). For the dancers in *Miss Lina's Ballerinas and the Prince*, the trophy is not a tutu but being selected to dance with a male dance partner, a signal to the audience that the chosen ballerina is the best among the female dancers in the group. Upon hearing that a male dancer is being recruited for the end of year recital, the girls think, "To dance with a prince in her first 'pas de deux' would be very special, each one of them knew" (Maccarone & Davenier, 2011, 7).

Tucker, unlike Tallulah, Rosie, Miss Lina's ballerinas, and the Swan Princess, is not concerned with material rewards such as a tutu, a pair of satin pointe shoes, or a trophy partner. Instead, he covets recognition of his dancing body as legitimate—as a permissible, appropriate, and acceptable type of active body for a boy. For example, "When Tucker brings the dessert bowls to the table with a ronde de jambe, Uncle Frank shakes his head, looks at Tucker's mother and says, 'You ought to put that boy in football.' Sometimes that bothers Tucker, so he finds an excuse to cabriole over to his mom" (Gruska & Wummer, 2011, 10–11). The ridicule and teasing that Tucker must overcome as a male ballet dancer reiterates the notion that boys tend to evaluate a successful sporting body in terms of performing masculinity (Drummond, 2003).

When Tucker's troubles are juxtaposed against Tallulah and Rosie's frustration at not immediately being recognized as the most beautiful ballerinas in the class, the girls appeared shallow. Moreover, this portrayal suggests the female dancing body is one to be taken less seriously since practice and perfection are portrayed as a means to an end. As I noted earlier, the protagonist in *Tallulah's Tutu* is fixated on wearing a beautiful tutu. Because she already perceives herself to be "an excellent ballerina," she is convinced that "soon, I'll get a tutu" (Singer & Boiger, 2011, 6). Tallulah's acceptance of the need to practice many hours before earning her tutu suggests that dancing is not an end in itself, but rather a means to become a perfect ballerina worthy of her beautiful tutu. In contrast, across the books, there is no association between the level of accomplishment and type of clothing male dancers wore. I now turn to a related theme: the lone male dancer.

The Lone Male Dancer
Five of the six books analyzed include a male dancer (Gruska & Wummer, 2007; Holub & McNicholas, 2012; Mayhew, 2011; Singer &

Boiger, 2011; Maccarone & Davenier, 2011). In addition to being rendered visible on account of his central position at the ballet barre, and his ideal position as male lead, the lone male dancer is also marked by the type of movements he performs (Adams, 2005). These include, but are not limited to, large, energetic, and athletic movements such as leaps, dives, and lunges as well as small, precise movements such as plié and ronde de jambe. In contrast to Tallulah in *Tallulah's Tutu*, who is reprimanded for taking up too much space, the boy in *Miss Linas's Ballerinas and the Prince* covers a great deal of space: "He took three big steps, then bounced off the floor, did a split in the air, and he soared out the door!" (Maccarone & Davenier, 2011, 15–19). Unlike the girls in this story, the boy's movements were not confined to a grid formation composed of nine bodies dancing in unison, three by three.

When male dancers perform the same movement alongside female dancers, both the written and visual texts suggest that the male dancer perform with more strength and athleticism. Curry, Arriagada, and Cornwell (2002) draw similar conclusions, noting that media images depict male athletes engaged in "power and performance sport activities" (408). For example, in *The Only Boy in Ballet Class*, one scene depicts Tucker, between two female dancers, jumping higher and faster than his female counterparts. In addition to the visuals, the language used to articulate movements performed by female dancers conjures images of smaller, less energetic, and quieter movements. For instance, in *Tallulah's Tutu*, Tallulah's movements are described as follows: "She turned out her feet and curved her hands near her hips in first position. She bent her knees in a plié" (Singer & Boiger 2012, 5). The written and visual text here compare and differentiate the boy and girl's ballet body, producing a particular truth-effect that contributes to the normalization of the body as gendered. In another example, when the boy from *Miss Lina's Ballerinas and the Prince* realizes that he will be dancing with girls, he remarks, "Dancing with girls was not at all fun" (Maccarone & Davenier, 2011, 15). With this statement, he reproducea the binary logic in which girls are constructed as other (weaker, less athletic). Likewise, the girls reject this boy's energetic and athletic style, dismissing him as arrogant.

Like the boy from *Miss Lina's Ballerinas and the Prince*, Tucker, the protagonist in *The Only Boy in Ballet Class*, reifies understandings of the male dancer as athletic (Adams, 2005). When asked to fill in for an absent football player, Tucker out-maneuvers his opponents and single-handedly wins the football championship, demonstrating that he is as athletic as any football player on the field (Gruska & Wummer, 2007, p.18). As a result of the specialized footwork, flexibility, and agility he developed in his ballet class, Tucker is the envy of every football player on the field. However, the male ballet body as an end in itself is neither celebrated nor endorsed as the acceptable or appropriate body for a boy. On the contrary, the ballet body is viewed as a body in transition waiting to morph into that of a star football player (Adams, 2005).

To summarize, my Foucauldian analysis resulted in three major themes across the books. First, the ballet body is portrayed with a slim build and slender arms and legs, often with a slightly protruding tummy and large head in proportion to the rest of the body. All of the protagonists' bodies are represented in this manner. Second, the representation of the bodies is gendered: female protagonists engage with clothing and physical appearance, whereas the male protagonist focuses on the performance. The male protagonists face problems and experience success at a group or team level, whereas female protagonists tend to deal with issues at an individual level. For example, when Tallulah and Rosie dream of tutus and pointe shoes, Tucker uses his flexibility to win a football championship (Ferguson & Goode, 2012; Gruska & Wummer, 2007; Singer & Boiger, 2011). Third, the ballet body is disciplined and then achieves success, happiness, and acceptance by others. For example, while Tucker is accepted and celebrated for his football performances, the ballerinas have to work hard to earn tutus, pointe shoes, or the coveted role of prima ballerina (Ferguson & Goode, 2012; Gruska & Wummer, 2007; Maccarone & Davenier, 2011; Singer & Boiger, 2011).

Conclusion

The purpose of employing discourse analysis was to understand how certain types of bodies are rendered visible, while others are rendered less visible, thereby producing a truth-effect in regards to the type of body that is appropriate, acceptable, and permissible as a ballet body during childhood. Foucault's theorization of power/knowledge operating through discourse to produce a truth-effect affords the space required to problematize how a discourse of aesthetics, operating within a sample of children's picture books, produces meanings of the ballet body. It is not surprising that a discourse of aesthetics dominates, given the highly gendered and stereotypical representations of boys' and girls' ballet bodies portrayed across the six books.

As noted, the ideal dancing body is (1) similar in terms of appearance (e.g., shape and size, able-bodied, fair skin); (2) gendered; and (3) disciplined. Foucault (1977) would argue that the images (appearance, shape, and size of the body) available to the reader are both a producer and a product of truth. More specifically, the narrow range of images (re)produce a particular truth about the type of body that is acceptable, appropriate, and permissible in these texts: "In short, it normalizes" understandings of the body (183). Body shapes and sizes that differ from the "norm" are excluded, thereby (re)producing these absent or "forbidden" bodies as unacceptable, inappropriate, and impermissible (Foucault, 1977, 183). As Markula and Pringle (2006) explain, the process of exclusion functions as a disciplinary technique in that it conveys understandings of the "correct" type of body, in this case, for a dancing child. The correct body is rewarded by its presence in the texts, whereas the incorrect body is punished by its absence (Matthews, 2009). Absent bodies include those with a disability as well as overweight bodies.

The emphasis on beauty connects to wider understandings of gender and sport in which the accomplishments of female athletes are frequently conflated with references to their physical appearance in an attempt to feminize the female athlete (Adams,

2005; Cooky, 2011; Hilliard, 1984). Because the active female body is viewed as a potential threat to the natural gender order, participation that sanctions aggressive, assertive, and competitive behaviours tends to be denounced (e.g., Curry, Arriagada, & Cornwell, 2002; Duncan, 1990). Instead, behaviours and bodies that conform to dominant understandings of femininity are rewarded as beautiful and successful. Books such as *Tallulah's Tutu, Ballerina Rosie, Miss Lina's Ballerinas and the Prince, Ballet Stars* and *Ella Bella Ballerina and Swan Lake* reproduce a particular truth-effect that, in turn, sustains a power-relation in which the ideal female body continues to be constructed in opposition to the ideal male body. Ultimately, the correct "look" for the female dancing body is one that reproduces traditional understandings of femininity. By conforming to this ideal, young girl ballet dancers are complicit in the maintenance of a power dynamic in which they are produced as "other" in relation to boys.

Within a neoliberal context the emphasis on looking good promotes the individual's responsibility to produce (e.g., work ethic) and consume (e.g., health and beauty products/services) (Garrett, 2004; Maguire, 2001; Markula, 2001). Normalizing the dancing body as beautiful at an early age increases the potential that girls will strive to maintain this image as the body ages: a tutu, a tiara, or a pair of pointe shoes will not suffice. Instead, the female body will require a host of products and services to look good. Thus, the books discipline girls to focus on physical beauty and to adopt behaviours and practices, which not only render them more compliant and easier to manage, but also make them associate beauty with the acquisition of material objects and the need to work to support the ongoing process of body work.

The emphasis on strength and athleticism has the potential to convey a similar message to male readers, encouraging them from an early age to invest both time and energy developing the correct work ethic in order to develop the correct shape and size of body. In these ways, the books analyzed here plant the idea of how the ideal ballet body should look and behave in the larger context of how we know about gender relations in contemporary society.

Note

1. A fluid understanding of self differentiates Foucault from the critical theorists who understand the self as ideologically constructed and fixed within a set binary, such as oppressed-oppressor. Foucault's understanding of the self as fluid and always involved in relations of power affords the potential to change the power dynamic by changing oneself.

References

Adams, M. (2005). "Death to the prancing prince": Effeminacy, sport discourses and the salvation of men's dancing. *Body & Society*, 11(4), 63–86.

Bettle, N., Bettle, O., Neumarker, U., & Neumarker, K. (2001). Body image and self-esteem in adolescent ballet dancers. *Perceptual & Motor Skills*, 93(1), 297–309.

Boyd, J. (2004). Dance, culture, and popular film. *Feminist Media Studies*, 4(1), 67–83.

Cooky, C. (2011). Do girls rule? Understanding popular culture images of girl power and sport. In S. Prettyman & B. Lampman (Eds.), *Learning culture through sports* (210–26). Lanham, MD: Rowman & Littlefield.

Curry, T. J., Arriagada, P. A., & Cornwell, B. (2002). Images of sport in popular non-sport magazines: Power and performance versus pleasure and participation. *Sociological Perspectives*, 45, 397–413.

Dittmar, H., Halliwell, E., & Ive, S. (2006). Does Barbie make girls want to be thin? The effect of experimental exposure to images of dolls on the body image of 5- to 8-year-old girls. *Developmental Psychology*, 42(2), 283–92.

Dohnt, H. K., & Tiggemann, M. (2008). Promoting positive body image in young girls: An evaluation of "Shapesville." *European Eating Disorders Review*, 16(3), 222–33.

Drummond, M. (2003). The meaning of boys' bodies in physical education. *The Journal of Men's Studies*, 11, 131–43.

Duncan, M. (1990). Sports photographs and sexual difference: Images of women and men in the 1984 and 1988 Olympic Games. *Sociology of Sport Journal*, 7, 22–43.

Ferguson, S., & Goode, D. (2012). *Ballerina Rosie*. New York: Simon and Schuster.

Foucault, M. (1972). *The archaeology of knowledge and the discourse on language*. (A. M. Sheridan Smith, Trans.). New York: Pantheon Books.

Foucault, M. (1977). *Discipline and punish: The birth of the prison*. (A. Sheridan, Trans.). London: Vintage Books.

Foucault, M. (1980). *Power and knowledge: Selected interviews and other writings, 1972–1977*. C. Gordon (Ed.). C. Gordon, L. Marshall, J. Mepham, & K. Soper (Trans.). New York: Pantheon Books.

Garrett, R. (2004). Negotiating a physical identity: Girls, bodies, and physical education. *Sport, Education, and Society, 9*, 223–37.

Gruska, D., & Wummer, A. (2007). *The only boy in ballet class*. Layton, UT: Gibbs Smith.

Hamdi, R., & Newbery, E. (2004). Bottoms, bodies, and blood. *Interpretation Journal, 9*(2), 8–10.

Hamilton, M.C., Anderson, D., Broaddus, M., & Young, K. (2006). Gender stereotyping and under-representation of female characters in 200 popular children's picture books: A twenty-first century update. *Sex Roles, 55*, 757–65.

Hemming, P. (2007). Renegotiating the primary school: Children's emotional geographies of sport, exercise, and active play. *Children's Geographies, 5*(4), 353–71.

Hilliard, D. C. (1984). Media images of male and female professional athletes: An interpretive analysis of magazine articles. *Sociology of Sport Journal, 1*, 251–62.

Holub, J., & McNicholas, S. (2012). *Ballet stars*. New York: Random House.

Hunt, P. (1985). Necessary misreadings: Directions in narrative theory for children's literature. *Studies in the Literary Imagination, 18*, 107–21.

Hunter, M. G. (1982). Fair play: The girl athlete in young adult fiction, 1900–1980 [Abstract]. *North American Society For Sport History Proceedings & Newsletter*, 16–17.

Kadel, N. J., Donaldson-Fletcher, E. A., Gerberg, L. F., & Micheli, L. J. (2005). Anthropometric measurements of young ballet dancers. *Journal of Dance Medicine & Science, 9*(3/4), 84–90.

Kane, M. J. (1998). Fictional denials of female empowerment: A feminist analysis of young adult sports fiction. *Sociology of Sport Journal, 15*, 231–62.

Maccarone, G., & Davenier, C. (2011). *Miss Lina's ballerinas and the prince*. Dongguan City, GD: South China Printing.

Maguire, J. (2001). Fit and flexible: The fitness industry, personal trainers and emotional service labor. *Sociology of Sport Journal, 18*, 379–402.

Markula, P. (2001). Beyond the perfect body: Women's body image distortion in fitness magazine discourse. *Journal of Sport & Social Issues, 25*, 158–79.

Markula, P., & Pringle, R. (2006). *Foucault, sport and exercise: Power, knowledge and transforming the self*. New York: Routledge.

Markula, P., & Silk, M. (2011). *Qualitative methods for physical culture*. New York: Palgrave Macmillan.

Matthews, N. (2009). Contesting representations of disabled children in picture-books: Visibility, the body and the social model of disability. *Children's Geographies, 7*(1), 37–49.

Mayhew, J. (2011). *Ella bella ballerina and Swan Lake*. New York: Barron's Educational Series.

Miskec, J. M. (2014). Pedi-files: Reading the foot in contemporary illustrated children's literature. *Children's Literature*, 42(1), 224–45.

Moller, A., & Masharawi, Y. (2011). The effect of first ballet classes in the community on various postural parameters in young girls. *Physical Therapy in Sport*, 12(4), 188–93.

Nilges, L. M., & Spencer, A. F. (2002). The pictorial representation of gender and physical activity level in Caldecott medal winning children's literature (1940–1999): A relational analysis of physical culture. *Sport, Education and Society*, 7, 135–50.

Oliver, W. (2005). Reading the ballerina's body: Susan Bordo sheds light on Anastasia Volochkova and Heidi Guenther. *Dance Research Journal*, 37(2), 38–54.

Paterson, S. B., & Lach, M. A. (1990). Gender stereotypes in children's books: Their prevalence and influence on cognitive and affective development. *Gender and Education*, 2(2), 185–97.

Pickard, A. (2013). Ballet body belief: Perceptions of an ideal ballet body from young ballet dancers. *Research in Dance Education*, 14, 3–19.

Rogers, J. (2008). Picturing the child in nineteenth-century literature: The artist, the child, and a changing society. *Children and Libraries: The Journal of the Association for Library Service to Children*, 6(3), 41–46.

Rogers, R., & Christian, J. (2007). "What could I say?": A critical discourse analysis of the construction of race in children's literature. *Race, Ethnicity and Education*, 19(1), 21–46.

Saric, J. (2005). Collapsing the disciplines: Children's literature, children's culture, and Andrew O'Malley's *The Making of the Modern Child*. *Pedagogy*, 5(3), 500–09.

Sherlock, J. (1991). Culture, ideology, gender and dance/Culture, ideologie, sexe et danse. *Society & Leisure/Loisir & Société*, 14(2), 543–56.

Singer, M., & Boiger, A. (2011). *Tallulah's tutu*. New York: Clarion Books.

Singleton, E. (2004). Grace and Dorothy: Collisions of femininity and physical activity in two early twentieth-century book series for girls. *Children's Literature in Education*, 35(2), 113–34.

Stallcup, J. E. (2004). Inescapable bodies, disquieting perception: Why adults seek to tame and harness Swift's excremental satire in Gulliver's travels. *Children's Literature in Education*, 35(2), 87–111.

Stokić, E., Srdić, B., & Barak, O. (2005). Body mass index, body fat mass and the occurrence of amenorrhea in ballet dancers. *Gynecological Endocrinology*, 20(4), 195–99.

Stott, J. C. (1979). Biographies of sport heroes and the American dream. *Children's Literature in Education*, 10 (4), 174–85.

Turk, M. (2014). Girlhood, ballet, and the cult of the tutu. *Children's Literature*, 39, 482–505.

Wainwright, S. P., Williams, C., & Turner, B. S. (2007). Globalization, habitus, and the balletic body. *Cultural Studies/Critical Methodologies*, 7, 308–25.

Weiller, K. H., & Higgs, C. T. (1989). Female learned helplessness in sport: An analysis of children's literature. *Journal of Physical Education, Recreation & Dance, 60*(6), 65–67.

Worland, J. (2008). Girls will be girls...and so on: Treatment of gender in preschool books from 1960 through 1990. *Children & Libraries: The Journal of the Association for Library Service to Children, 6* (1), 42–46.

2

SO YOU THINK YOU CAN DANCE

The Feminine Ballet Body in a Popular Reality Show

Pirkko Markula

Although television is now facing serious competition from other screens and programming options, formatted reality shows still draw audiences. Similar to sport (Bonner, 2013), these shows invariably involve some type of competition or contest to determine a winner at the end of the season. Performing arts have also jumped on the reality television bandwagon. Music, particularly singing, has provided the main premise for such hugely popular talent reality shows as *American Idol, The Voice,* and *Got Talent.* Even dance, often a less publicly visible performing art,[1] has succeeded in attracting large audiences through reality formats. In 2015, *Dancing with the Stars* (DWTS) had an average audience of fifteen million and *So You Think You Can Dance* (SYTYCD) five million viewers.[2] Both programs have been credited with increasing the awareness of dance among mainstream audiences.

Although ballet is arguably the most visible and most financially supported theatrical dance form in the Westernized world,[3] it seldom appears in these dance reality shows. There are, however, ballet dancers among the SYTYCD contestants, and in this chapter,

I examine how ballet is constructed in the popularized, commercialized mediascape of the Canadian version of SYTYCD, which aired four seasons from 2008 to 2011 on CTV.[4] Before introducing my Deleuzian theoretical framework, I discuss previous literature that locates gendered dancing bodies within the context of reality talent shows.

Dance and Dancing Bodies within Reality Dance Shows

Despite their popularity, dance reality shows have attracted a modest amount of scholarship, much of which focuses on DWTS (e.g., Bonner, 2013; Butler, Mocarski, Emmons, & Smallwood, 2014; Enli, 2009; McMains, 2010; Quinlan & Bates, 2008). In her insightful work, Bonner analyzes the role of the celebrities, rather than the professional dancers, in the success of the DWTS/*Strictly Come Dancing* in Australia, the United States, and the UK. One central aspect of the show, she argues, is the hard labour, including humiliation, of the celebrities learning to dance. During the show, background narratives assign each contestant a role as either an incompetent "sore-thumb" celebrity who lacks all qualities of a dancer, or as a contestant transformed from an inexperienced to a confident performer (see also Butler et al., 2014). Other scholars have focused on the representation of a particular celebrity to argue that the dance shows reproduce popular stereotypes of gender (Butler et al., 2014) and disability (Quinlan & Bates, 2008). Research on SYTYCD follows similar themes, but instead of focusing on celebrities, this research focuses on professional dancers who compete against each other in the show.

Elswit (2012), a dance studies scholar, observes that SYTYCD "does not privilege movement," dance skill, or choreographic complexity; rather, "the show teaches audiences that engagement with dance is structured by dance's theatrical mechanisms, and allows for moments of strong feeling because of, rather than despite, those mechanisms" (134). This type of dance, which she labels "dance-that-is-not-about-dance" (136), embodies the affective potentiality of theatricality: the audience learns how to feel dance, not through dance movement per se, but through other theatrical elements such as costuming, music, staging, lights, and, particularly, various narratives constructed throughout the show. These stories include the judges' comments, the stories told through the different choreographies, and the pre-performance stories from rehearsals. These narratives, while seemingly separate from each other, make "viewers to be aware of tensions, like those between the dancers as people and the dance roles they perform" (Elswit, 2012, 140). The pre-performance clips frequently show the dancers failing difficult maneuvers, and thus, like DWTS, draw attention to the hard labour of learning dance that, to the audience, appears effortless when on the stage. These techniques, Elswit (2012) indicates, allow the audience to experience a feeling response to the difficulty of dance and the story told in the choreographed performance. When the usually invisible aspects preceding the dance performance (rehearsals, the choreographic process) become visible, they elicit strong feelings that then carry the show to a large audience that is not necessarily educated in dance movement.

In addition to the narrative lines, other scholars have focused on analyzing how individual dancers have been represented in SYTYCD. Although the vast majority of dancers are women (according to the Canada Council for Arts [2004], 85 per cent of Canadian dancers are women), SYTYCD gives an impression of a more equal gender representation with ten men and ten women finalists. In fact, the male dancers have evoked more scholarly attention. Broomfield (2011), for example, illustrates the construction of hegemonic masculinity through an incident in the first season of the American version of SYTYCD. The head judge, Nigel Lythgoe, accused a young, black male dancer, Anthony Bryant, of "not dancing masculine" when using a ribbon in a choreography that Lythgoe compared to a "Russian gymnastics routine in the Olympics." The concern with the lack of masculinity, according to Broomfield (2011), indicates a failure to confront homosexuality and effeminacy as aspects of dance. Male dancers' identity construction in the US version of SYTYCD also intrigued Quail (2011), who examined two white men, the 2006 finalists, Benji Swimmer and Travis Wall, dancing a duet where they transformed from "nerds" to cool hip-hop dudes and back to "sexless" nerds, a plot that Quail (2011) found reifying "the hypersexualization of black masculinity and compulsory African American cool" (469). In this sense, reality dance shows can be argued to reproduce popular male stereotypes according to which men engage in strength moves (e.g., lifting the females) and/or certain types of dance genres (e.g., hip hop/house/ krump). The stereotypes of male dancers, however, tend to be opposite to the hegemonic masculinity that is exemplified, for example, by many male team sport players (e.g., American football, rugby, basketball, baseball). Broomfield (2011) argues that SYTYCD needs to educate American audiences that are still unsettled by "the stigma of gayness and effeminacy attached to male dancers" (124). Risner (2009) notes that, indeed, gay men make up a significant number of male dancers. If the ballerina is a deeply stereotypical and narrow representation of femininity, all dance forms, including ballet, also reproduce stereotypes of male effeminacy that limit how we understand dance and dancing bodies (Burt, 2007; Fisher & Shay, 2009; Gard, 2008; Risner, 2009). Such analyses have illuminated the potential of dance as supporting or resisting dominant cultural identity construction (Elswit, 2012). In this chapter, I am also interested in how two individual female ballet dancers—and through them, ballet as a dance form—appear in the show.

Many feminist researchers consider ballet, of all the theatrical dance forms, to align closest with traditional femininity. They argue that the image of a ballet dancer, through her movements (extensions, weightlessness, a sense of etherealness, the arch of the foot and the back, the turn-out, the upwardness of the chest), size (petite, light, delicate), and costuming (fitted leotard, the tutu that displays the crotch and legs, low-cut tops), reproduces the discourse of patriarchal dominance (Aalten, 2005; Adair, 1992; Boyd, 2004; Thomas, 2003; Wulff, 1998). This aesthetic emphasizes the look of the body, and thus necessitates an extreme focus on body care. In addition, ballerinas' roles (fairies and swans) divide women dualistically into good and evil, created to attract men's attention (Foster, 1996). At the same time, these female characters assure a stoic and potent male identity for the partnering male dancers or the male audience members. The ballet technique where the male is primarily lifting or handling the erect, responsive ballerina, whose technical skill focuses on creating harmonious lines of her extended limbs, emphasizes the sexual difference between the male and female, a difference that is perceived as a natural, biological necessity: the stronger male lifts and directs the feeble and relatively passive female (Daly, 1987; Foster, 1996; Wulff, 1998). This emphasis effectively serves to separate women from men and creates the ballerina as an object for the male audience's desiring gaze (Adair, 1992; Foster, 1996).

If this is, indeed, the dominant feminine identity in theatrical high-art ballet, how might this representation resonate with ballet in the SYTYCD context of commercial media? Instead of engaging in the debates of hegemonic identity construction in SYTYCD, I have chosen to use a poststructuralist Deleuzian perspective in an attempt to see if it is possible to move beyond the hyper-feminization of ballet dancers in this popular dance show.

The "Face" of Ballet

I employ the Deleuzian concept of "face" to map how individual ballet dancers gain a recognizable identity within the intersections of a commercially driven reality show format and the performing art of ballet. "Face is produced," Deleuze and Guattari (1987) explain, "when the body, head included, has been decoded and has been overcoded by something we shall call the Face" (170). They further emphasize that "faces are not basically individual: they define zones of frequency or probability, delimit the field that neutralizes in advance any expressions or connections unamenable to the appropriate significations" (168). In the late capitalist societies, the appreciated signification of the "face" is aligned with a binary dualistic scheme (e.g., masculine/feminine, white/black, art/popular culture, expressive/technical, emotional/rational, sweet/sexy, beautiful/ugly), and an individual is clearly positioned on either side of the binary divide. For example, in SYTYCD, the dancers' faces can be clearly constructed as socially recognizable as "girls" or "guys," as ballet dancers or ballroom dancers, through certain movement vocabulary and language use.

As it continues to emerge with late capitalism (Lorraine, 2008), this binary definition reduces the complexity of one's embodied existence "to what can be captured and coded through the faces that are socially recognizable...and psychically convincing" (84). Deleuze and Guattari (1987) add, "certain assemblages of power (*pouvoir*) require the production of a face" (175) that is then reinforced through, for example, the close-up shots in popular television shows. For instance, a female dancer might be represented as continually repeating the same "personalised patterns of meaning and behaviour" (Lorraine, 2008, 63) appropriate to ballet. Following Elswit (2012), the emotional narratives of the show might make her face even more psychically convincing.

For Deleuze and Guattari (1987), then, the face is an "affair of" the organization of power and, as such, they attest, "the face has a great future, but only if it is destroyed, dismantled" (175). Lorraine (2009) further observes that "whether one lives out these designations and interpellations in comfortable conformity or painful dissonance depends upon whether the multiple forces... resonate with dominant memory...(sanctioned by the mainstream) or induce...counter-memories" (65). Mass media such as television can effectively transmit dominant memories, but also engage counter-memories of ballet. Deleuze and Guattari (1987) remark, indeed, that the power of television lies in the efficacy of ciphering "the face," and thus, they conclude, it is also "an affair of economy" (175) that engenders the concrete, individual face. In what follows, I now analyze how the televised face of ballet in the popular reality dance show SYTYCD might engender individual ballet dancers' personalized patterns.

The Ballet Face in SYTYCD

SYTYCD is a part of the assemblage of professional dance (the participants are trained dancers), and thus its face is made primarily recognizable through dance styles that are then characterized by certain facial traits. For example, the main judges, Luther Brown (hip hop), Blake McGrath (contemporary), Tré Armstrong (tap, video), Jean-Marc Généreux (ballroom) all represent different dance styles, but are also carefully selected to equally signify both sides of other socially recognizable, majoritarian binaries (black/white, men/women, anglo/francophone). The twenty mostly white dancers compete as individuals against each other in various styles in short dance pieces designed by professional choreographers with experience mainly in show business or television.[5] The judges all serve as choreographers, but somewhat stereotypically, black choreographers (Tré Armstrong, Tanisha Scott, Jae Blaze, Lil'C, Luther Brown, Sho-Tyme, Flii Stylz) create exclusively hip-hop, krump, and house pieces.[6]

Unlike theatrical professional ballet, the SYTYCD face is recognizable by a trait of competition similar to dance sport. In addition, engendered by dominant memory of both ballet and dance sport, male/female partnering is its dominant feature: the contestants perform primarily as couples. In this sense, the face of SYTYCD shares a trait with the traditional face of theatrical ballet where the stronger male is assigned to lift the lithe ballerina (Daly, 1987; Foster, 1996; Wulff, 1998). This partnership is fixed (unless one of the dancers was eliminated), but after the fifth week the dancers are required to switch partners in each consequent episode to showcase their versatility and adaptability in new situations. In the competitive context of SYTYCD, another important feature of a good dancer is the ability to perform a variety of dance styles (from ballroom to hip hop) according to a previously unknown script (the choreography was created anew for each performance).

In this context, only two women ballet dancers appeared among the top twenty dancers during the four seasons of the Canadian SYTYCD: Allie Bertram in season one and Corynne Barron in season two.[7] They shared many similarities. Both were from Alberta: Bertram from Calgary and Barron from Edmonton. Both were eighteen years old and thus among the youngest competitors in SYTYCD. They also differed in several ways. At five feet tall, Bertram self-identified as "a ballet dancer from Calgary," with "dancing on pointe" as her signature move. She also recalled starting "dancing at a community centre" and "only did ballet" (Lewis, 2008). She graduated from the International School of Ballet and also had some professional experience as a dancer with the Boston Ballet (Market News Publishing, 2008). If Bertram's face as a ballerina was strongly identifiable from the beginning of the season, Barron's face was more difficult to recognize. Having trained with the Edmonton School of Ballet and the Royal Winnipeg Ballet School, she reported participating also in contemporary and jazz ("CTV's Top 20," 2009) and was described as "a classical contemporary dancer" (Sperounes, 2009). It was further revealed that she was "a late bloomer in the world of ballet"; while she started ringette at five, she began dancing at age fourteen (Sperounes, 2009). Although Barron explained that "When the time came to choose (between ballet and ringette), it was dance 100 per cent...My heart is in dance" (Sperounes, 2009, B1), her career as a ringette goalie was constantly highlighted in the show. For example, the introductory shot presented Barron's ringette coach, her dad, as her biggest fan. Her face, thus, tended to be structured based on traits from sport, ballet, and contemporary dance.

The biggest difference between the two dancers was their success in the show: Bertram made the final, losing to the first season's winner, contemporary dancer Nico Archambault, whereas Barron was eliminated in week five without being selected among the top ten competitors. Regardless of these differences, a recognizable "face of ballet" emerged through the representation of these dancers. I now discuss the features of the ballet face shared by Allie and Corynne, as they were referred to during the show, before examining how they further illuminated the commercially mediated, popular dance face of SYTYCD.

The Nice Face of Ballet

The ballet face was constructed by repeatedly signifying the two ballet dancers' personalities, their bodies, and their movement vocabularies as "traits" of a ballerina. While there were differences between the two dancers, these were highlighted against the same main features.

Because SYTYCD presents Canada's "favourite dancer" (not the best or most skilled dancer), the contestants need to display attributes other than their dance abilities. Therefore, a clearly distinguishable, attractive personality could draw audience votes. Allie as a person emerged as "adorable," an angel and sweetheart with a lovely smile and an infectious laugh. "Allie, the ballerina," was further affixed with identifiers such as "bella," "cute-as-a-button," "little girl," "Princess," or "little Miss." Such terms further infantilized the eighteen-year-old Allie, who was indeed the youngest competitor in the first season. These girlish traits, rather than Allie as an individual, came to characterize the ballet face in season one. In season two, Corynne, who was the same age as Allie and also the youngest performer, together with eighteen-year-old jazz dancer Jenna-Lynn Higgins, was not identified by her age, but, like Allie, she was referred to as "little miss happy face" or "little girl," and was characterized as "always giggling." She was, however, most commonly addressed through relatively standard terms referring to her performance ("beautiful," "nice," "good," "elegant") and, most notably, her body.

From the beginning of the finals, Corynne was said to "have the legs." She even introduced herself by wanting to "not just be the dancer with legs." Her first performance, a Viennese waltz, provided her a chance to "not overtly us[e] her legs" and let "other skills rise," according to judge Jean-Marc Généreux. Similarly, judge Tré Armstrong acknowledged Corynne's "potential as a dancer... far outreach[ed] any talk" of her legs in her contemporary performance, but Armstrong immediately proceeded to praise the perfect extensions of Corynne's legs and her faultless, pointed toes. Guest judge Karen Kain (an ex-prima ballerina and artistic director of the National Ballet of Canada) also remarked on Corynne's legs: "Everybody talks about your legs. I have nicknamed you 'Miss Legs Girl.' They are very beautiful, but also very expressive." Long, lean legs have previously been noted as the signature feature of the perfect ballerina (Aalten, 2005; Thomas, 2003; Wulff, 1998), and thus the constant referral to Corynne's legs clearly allocated her the socially recognizable face of ballet. Allie's ballet face was not defined through a particular body part, but rather her body size.

Physically, "little miss" Allie was indeed small. The audience was reminded of her petite size through telling moments such as the rehearsal footage from her Viennese waltz with Nico Archambault, who effortlessly lifted Allie and repeatedly exclaimed, "she is so small." Instead of highlighting Allie's petite frame, the judges focused on her technical ability, which they attributed to ballet training. During the show, it was revealed that Allie's dancing ability impressed the judges in her audition, during which she performed a ballet routine that included her favourite moves: high grand jeté and a series of fouetté pirouettes. For example, judge Blake McGrath remembered the audition judges unanimously moving Allie to the two-week preliminary elimination phase to Las Vegas where the final twenty dancers were determined. Interestingly, Allie was most commonly involved in ballroom dance style routines (jive, mambo, quickstep, Viennese waltz, samba), and the judges also picked her mambo and jive performances as their favourites for the final show. During these performances, the judges nevertheless praised Allie's ballet-like characteristics: her lines during the lifts, the effortlessness, her feet. Such praise was possible because, as Rex Harrington, one of the show's judges and an artist-in-residence with the National Ballet of Canada, explained as he praised Allie's "beautiful facility," with a ballet background "you can do everything," to which Allie responded with wholehearted agreement and exclaimed, "it helps with everything!"

Corynne was also given a ticket to Las Vegas without any hesitation. While Corynne's appearance in the show was much shorter, she performed in a variety of dances, including Viennese waltz, Paso Doble, salsa, jazz, and contemporary. Her contemporary piece was nominated as the judges' favourite for the final show. Like Allie, Corynne's technical ability was praised through her appearance, and Rex Harrington, who had "a soft spot for all ballerinas," openly compared her to Allie: "Like Allie last year, I do love you... You have such an amazing facility to work with." Despite their "amazing" technical ability, both Allie and Corynne were among the bottom three performers who had to "dance for their lives" in solo performances to stay on the show.

Corynne danced two solos in bare feet, using movement vocabulary that could have been from contemporary dance. She openly displayed her strengths: high leg extensions, arabesques, high ronde de jambes, grand jetés spiced with different types of pirouettes. Her ballet face was recognizable in her first solo in which she wore a white tutu, which was also featured in the show's opening shots.

Allie's ballet face became more socially recognizable during her solo performances. Donning a traditional tutu and pointe shoes, she resorted to very traditional ballet performance of a pre-choreographed sequence from the traditional ballet Don Quixote (Act 1), after a hip-hop performance in week five landed her in among the bottom three dancers. Although Allie made several mistakes and hurt her ankle during the solo dance, the judges praised her for doing a pretty performance of a beautiful ballet. In her remaining self-choreographed solos, she continued to signify herself as a ballerina by wearing a tutu and pointe shoes, including a transitional piece in which she wore the pointe shoe on only one foot. Her ballet face was enhanced by these clearly identifiable and socially recognizable accessories. Although her choreography simulated the flow of contemporary dance (rather than still balances to celebrate and accentuate the lines of the body) with vocabulary outside of clearly identifiable ballet, all the solos incorporated her signature ballet moves (grand jetés, fouettés) in addition to spectacular high extensions, attitudes, and backbends inspired by gymnastics. In this sense, both Allie and Corynne's solo performances followed a similar line of a contemporary type of ballet that sustains the spectacular high extensions, jumps, and pirouettes, but adds level changes and floor work characteristic of contemporary dance.

Although the technical proficiency of both ballerinas obtained much praise, in a curious contradiction, the ballet face was further solidified by the constant assessment of their ability to step out of that genre. Consequently, a binary between a ballet face and a popularized commercial dance face was constructed in the show.

The Sexy, Emotional Face of Popularized Dance

Although Allie's face as a cute, little ballerina was sustained throughout the show, from the first week, there was a constant effort to transform her into something else. Already in the second episode, the choreographers emphasized their intention of changing her a into a sexy, sensual mambo dancer. Allie accepted the challenge, hoping to be able to expose her inner "tigress." According to judge Blake McGrath, the mambo performance successfully metamorphosed Allie to a "superhot" woman. She was then continually referred to as the chameleon that could make performing any dance form look effortless, and as an unbelievably versatile dancer who sizzled with energy and sexiness. After a hip-hop routine in episode eight, some of the judges gushed that Allie, who now was "getting it down and funky," had turned from Mary Poppins to "funkatrina." And, if she was not quite a "gansta" yet, she always gave the performance all she had, despite not being immediately comfortable with a new dance form. Although Allie was praised as the most transformed contestant, she had not entirely metamorphosed into a popular dance butterfly from her ballet cocoon: some of the judges continued to critique her for "not pulling off" the ballet face and urged her to push more to break out stylistically. At the same time, they continued to remind her not to forget her ballet roots as she moved to "street shoes."

Corynne received her chance to show a different side after the first week's Viennese waltz, which the judges found nice, beautiful, and good, but not particularly exciting. In the second week, she performed a Paso Doble in which she, like Allie the year before, hoped to reveal her "inner beast." Indeed, the judges found her now "giving emotionally," as Tré Armstrong put it, an essential feature of the popular dance face in SYTYCD. In the following week, her contemporary dance, which was choreographed by Stacey Tookey and examined an end of a relationship, exhibited her ability to engage emotionally even further. Judge Jean-Marc Généreux was moved to tears and the other judges praised Corynne for clearly "emoting" for the first time, in addition to having good technique. Généreux called Corynne "the new contemporary queen" with an ability to transform and emotionally unsettle the audience. Corynne later acknowledged, "I truly think my journey began with my contemporary piece with Stacey Tookey. She turned the tables for me. She made me realize that there is more to myself and she exposed me to Canada" (Angus, 2009, D10). At this point, Corynne's transformation appeared complete as she adopted the clearly recognizable face of a contemporary dancer, a winning face in popular dance shows.

Allie also performed two contemporary routines, which stood in stark contrast to both of her ballroom performances and her ballet solos because they emphasized the importance of a performer's ability to convey an emotional narrative through movement. Both contemporary dance choreographers loaded their pieces with moving narratives. The first conveyed lost and found love based on the choreographer's own story of her mother having to give her child, the choreographer's brother, up for adoption and then being reunited with her son twenty-six years later. The mom and newly discovered brother joined the audience for the performance.

Although designed to be emotionally charged, the choreography played on Allie's technical strengths by involving plenty of lifts, jumps, pirouettes, and showy extensions. Playing the role of the mom, Allie was praised for being able to "make the piece her own" and to express maturity and the emotionality of the story. Allie's second contemporary piece (also choreographed by Stacey Tookey and performed with Nico Archambault, the season's eventual winner) included an equally emotional story of a topical subject: a soldier having to leave his pregnant wife to enter a war zone. The choreography again showcased lifts that allowed Allie to display her beautiful lines. Unlike Corynne's contemporary performance, there was less reference to fulfilling any technical requirements of the piece and more concern of emotionality, spirituality, abandonment, and the connection between the two dancers—inspiration to the judges who were once again moved to tears. "Allie the ballerina" was repeatedly praised for her ability to step out of the highly technical execution of ballet movements to express the emotionality of contemporary dance. Therefore, Allie and Corynne's new faciality traits reflected the judges' and choreographers' intention of transforming them from the sweet, cute, technically good ballerinas into emotionally expressive contemporary dancers. While Allie excelled in emotional and sexy expression, Corynne struggled to convincingly display proper feminine sexuality.

After her transformation into the contemporary queen, who is able to emote properly, Corynne's pieces started to require more sexiness. In a jazz piece that placed Corynne in the role of "psycho stalker" with a "deadly obsession," she continued to be praised for her "clean and mean" technically good dancing, but her performance in the show finished with a salsa that required her to "be pretty hot" and perform "lots of pelvis thrusting" and "open legs." The judges juxtaposed her ballet technique ("an amazing ability of length," "always pulled up") with the requirements of salsa ("to pull down," to move the hips to express sexiness) to claim that, for a classical dancer, it is difficult "to move the hips" in the right direction. Corynne had not completely "owned" the popular dance face and, in judge Mia Michaels's words, displayed "the most forced sexiness" ever seen. According to judge Rex Harrington, Corynne had to continue to "find the truth" of the sexy salsa and "make it real."[8] Like Allie, Corynne had arrived to SYTYCD "as a little girl" and, to in Jean-Marc Généreux's assessment, "mature[d] very quickly to a young woman" who at least attempted to display feminine sexiness. In this sense, Corynne had fulfilled the main goals of SYTYCD: growing as a (sexy) dancer by trying different styles of dance. Although not entirely successful in her transformation, Corynne worked hard to improve her performance. Strong work ethic emerged as another essential feature of a SYTYCD face.

As Bonner (2013) and Elswit (2012) observe, reality dance shows emphasize the hard work of dance training, and the economic assemblage of SYTYCD that displays dance within the context of competition also embraces this faciality trait. Both Corynne and Allie were credited as working hard, but this trait was more pronounced in Allie's face as she reached the final. SYTYCD culminated in a finale that required the choreographers to create and rehearse the dancers in four different pieces within a week, in addition to the dancers having to provide a solo. When Allie reached this point of the show, the emphasis was on the taxing involvement of dance. The judges' commentary pointed to the exhaustion of and strain on the dancers' bodies and minds. Even the usually smiling Allie emphasized the hardship of the "mental aspect" as she broke down in tears during learning a jazz routine, an unfamiliar genre for her. True to its reality show format, the broadcast made the most of her breakdown, airing the emotional outburst before her actual performance. Therefore, the trait of hard work was intertwined with the trait of emotionality. As Elswit (2012) suggests, "SYTYCD trains audiences in affective dance spectatorship at the same time as it calls attention to the theatricality of dance as an art form" (136). Through this construction of the ballet face, SYTYCD viewers are taught to read dance through emotional engagement with the dancers' injuries, their pre-performance pressures, and the emotional narratives of the contemporary dance choreography especially.

Conclusion

Within the economic assemblage of SYTYCD, the face of ballet needed to be transformed for popular consumption. Instead of the upwardness, etherealness, and delicateness of a ballerina (Adair, 1992; Foster, 1996; Thomas, 2003; Wulff, 1998), the socially recognized faciality traits in this context were sexiness, emotionality, and hard work. Both ballet dancers were represented as struggling possibly more than the dancers from other genres, with the emotional and sexual expression necessarily for the popular, favourite, dance face. Consequently, they had to significantly adapt their ballet features. While their technical ability evoked awed admiration, the comments and advice on how to "truly" display being "hot" and "dirty" dominated the show. Allie wore the popular face more persuasively. Despite openly displaying her ballet background through her solos and ballet wardrobe (tutu and pointe shoes), she was crowned as the runner-up of Canada's first SYTYCD season. Corynne, on the other hand, remained a nice, technical dancer whose face was not recognized as a popular dancer or as a ballet dancer. After a successful display of emotionality characteristic of "the contemporary queen," she failed "to move her hips" convincingly for a sexy salsa. She was relegated back to a stiff, upright ballerina and then eliminated.

To paraphrase Lorraine (2008), each dancer could either live the designation of the SYTYCD face in comfortable conformity or painful dissonance. Where Corynne was seen needing more commitment to a real transformation, Allie gave her all to conform, and drew comfort from her technical ability as a ballerina to be able to resonate with the dominant memory of commercialized, popular, mass-mediated dance. While she had to compromise her ballet memory somewhat, Allie used it to survive the SYTYCD world that, oddly enough, kept referring to ballet in a contradictory discourse of admiration and "letting it go": the ballet face had an amazing facility, but one that needed more expression. Deleuze and Guattari (1987) observe, however, that faciality is not limited to an individual's facial expressions and feelings of successful conformity, but is, rather, an issue of "economy and the organization of power" (175).

Deleuze and Guattari (1987) remind us that the face is not individual; it is something that defines, delimits, or neutralizes in advance any expressions "unamenable to the appropriate significations" (168) of, in this case, dance in a capitalist society. The televised reality dance show amplifies this face through its closeups of the dancers' emotional faces, detailed focus on the judges' commentary, and the intimate rehearsal shots that all construct certain meanings through which we come to understand dance in popular culture. These meanings or significations then define which individual dancers should be successful competitors in an entertainment show. Allie and Corynne's "concrete faces" (Deleuze & Guattari, 1987, 168) were the walls from where various meanings of "Canada's most popular dancer" were "bounced off." Theirs were not "ready-made" faces (Deleuze & Guattari, 1987, 168), but had to be engendered to the specifications of the correct emotional sexiness for the commercial televised dance show. Deleuze and Guattari (1987) suggest that the appreciated signification of the face is aligned with a binary dualistic scheme (e.g., masculine/feminine, white/black, art/popular culture, expressive/technical, emotional/rational, sweet/sexy, beautiful/ugly), and an individual is clearly positioned on either side of the binary divide. Allie and Corynne's ballet dancer's face became recognizable as white, technical, and sweet. Paradoxically, their femininity was also constantly aligned with sexiness retained through the movement vocabulary (e.g., swinging hips, being lifted by the male dancers), emotional roles, and revealing clothing that constructed them as socially recognizable as dancing "girls."

It is evident that success in a televised reality dance show requires a production of a particularly kind of feminine face. Deleuze and Guattari (1987) would conclude that such a show is a part of the "abstract machine" or power that reproduces capitalist apparatus and defines the facial features of, among other individuals, the dancers. There is always a chance, they add, for "defacialization" (Deleuze & Guattari, 1987, 190), where the faciality traits are freed from their usual delimitation to exhibit different types of features. SYTYCD seems to define a dancer's face as distinct from a ballet face that several feminist researchers (e.g., Aalten, 2005; Adair, 1992; Boyd, 2004; Thomas, 2003; Wulff, 1998) find objectifying women through a reproduction of patriarchal dominance. But did the SYTYCD face alter the signifying traits indexed for a recognizable female dancer's face?

In the context of SYTYCD, the ballet memory was restored within the popular memory in a rather comfortable co-existence: both memories supported each other to deepen the gender binary of the technical but sexy, emotional, scantily clad female dancer lifted by the strong male dancer. Therefore, new counter-memories for the dominant themes of partner dancing were not generally endorsed in the popular reality show. In this assemblage, the moving body did not pave the "road to the asignifying and asubjective" (Deleuze & Guattari, 1987, 171), but was harnessed to support the dominant faciality traits that remained comfortably still. The popular dance face, then, continued to wear features that have made a female ballet dancer's face recognizable for decades: the emotional expressiveness of the prima ballerina (Karthas, 2012), the sexuality of the chorus dancer (Carter, 2005; Karthas, 2012), but also the technical ability and lean looks of the Balanchine ballerina (Morris, 2005). If popularizing dance through televised reality shows has not redefined the feminine dance face, it is time to consider other ways of dismantling its oppressive features for more diverse facial expressions of dance.

Author's Note

Research for this chapter was made possible through a Social Sciences and Humanities Research Council Canada research grant.

Notes

1. Historically, the most prominent form of dance media has been film, and thus a significant amount of research has focused on screen dance from Hollywood musicals to Bollywood to popular movies (e.g., *Dirty Dancing, Saturday Night Fever*), in which the characters dance. In her seminal text on dance in the media, Dodds (2001) divide "screen dance" into dance on screen (film), video dance, dance in television, and hybrid sites of (mediated) dance (see also Jordan & Allen, 2003; Mitoma, Zimmer, & Stieber, 2002). More recently, Reason and Reynolds (2010) advocate that all dance on screen could actually be understood as hybrid as it can no longer be characterized in a single term, but rather as a form in constant development and transition.

2. Unlike DWTS or its UK original, *Strictly Come Dancing*, SYTYCD does not involve non-dancing celebrities (the major draw card for DWTS) learning to dance, but is based on finding the favourite dancer among young (under thirty) trained, professional dancers. As an additional distinction, DWTS tends to focus on so-called ballroom dance styles, whereas SYTYCD includes a wider variety of dance styles from contemporary, hip hop, jazz, and Broadway to ballroom dance.

3. Boyd (2004) observed that American media dance narratives draw attention to the tensions between high culture and pop culture and function as reflections of upper and middle class, as well as racial and social divides. If the masses learn about dance through popular films and books, the "high art" performing arts (e.g., the opera or the ballet) are "traditionally favored by a culture's elite" (69). However, ballet as a privileged dance form that reflects "the ideological constructs of those in positions of power," significantly influences "culture's preferences for movement" (81).

4. The US version of SYTYCD aired during the summer starting in May after the finale of its sister show, *American Idol*. Both shows were produced by Simon Cowell and Nigel Lythgoe. Quail (2011) observes that summer is a fertile time for reality shows that are cheaper to produce than original drama but more popular than reruns. The US series was in its twelfth season in 2015 and was broadcast by FOX.

5. Season one featured one black woman, one black man, and one Latina dancer, but several francophone men, whereas season two featured one black man, one black woman, one Indian man, one Asian woman, and several francophones.

6. One black choreographer and guest judge, Sean Cheeseman, choreographed jazz and Broadway.

7. The third contestant who identified as a ballet dancer was Emanuel Sandhu (season two), who is best known as an international-level singles figure skater. Although a very interesting "face" in SYTYCD, the space is this chapter does not allow for a discussion of Sandhu's performance.

8. After Corynne's elimination, season two of SYTYCD *Canada* was noted for its overtly sexual choreography. For example, Debra Yeo in the *Toronto Star*

referred to the show as "kind of dirty. That's how I'd sum up *So You Think You Can Dance Canada* so far this season...We've had butt-grabbing, breast-brushing, grinding and shaking of very private parts in dancers' faces." While the guest US judge, Dan Karaty, encouraged such visible and free sexual expression—"Every time I see the show here in Canada it gets sexier and sexier. I love it, love it," he remarked—there were also critical voices. For example, in her SYTYCD blog for the *Montreal Gazette*, Kathryn Greenaway found the "routines...so oversexed they're doing damage to the show's family-viewing reputation," and cited several responses to her blog from concerned parents who no longer allowed their children to watch the show.

References

Aalten, A. (2005). In the presence of the body: Theorizing training, injuries and pain in ballet. *Dance Research Journal, 37*(2), 55–72.

Adair, C. (1992). *Women and dance: Sylphs and sirens.* New York: New York University Press.

Angus, K. (2009, September 25). "I finally believe in myself": Edmonton dancer sets her sights on making it big in Toronto. *Edmonton Journal,* D10.

Bonner, F. (2013). Celebrity, work and the reality-talent show: *Strictly Come Dancing/ Dancing with the Stars. Celebrity Studies, 4*(2), 169–81.

Boyd, J. (2004). Dance, culture, and popular film. *Feminist Media Studies, 4*(1), 67–83.

Broomfield, M. A. (2011). Policing masculinity and dance reality television: What gender nonconformity can teach in the classroom. *Journal of Dance Education, 11,* 124–28.

Burt, R. (2007). *The male dancer: Bodies, spectacle, sexualities.* London: Routledge.

Butler, S., Mocarski, R., Emmons, B., & Smallwood, R. (2014). Leaving it on the pitch: Hope Solo's negotiation of conflicting gender roles on *Dancing with the Stars. Journal of Gender Studies, 23,* 362–75.

Canada Council for Arts/Dance/Research (2004). Facts on dance: Then and now—and now what. Retrieved from http://www.CanadaCouncilforArts/Dance/Research

Carter, A. (2005). *Dance and dancers in the Victorian and Edwardian music hall ballet.* Hampshire and Burlington, UK: Ashgate.

CTV's So You Think You Can Dance Canada top 20 revealed. (2009). Retrieved from http://archive.newswire.ca/fr/story/507357/ctv-s-so-you-think-you-can-dance-canada-top-20-revealed

Daly, A. (1987). The Balanchine woman: Of hummingbirds and channel swimmers. *The Drama Review, 31,* 8–21.

Deleuze, G. & Guattari, F. (1987). *A thousand plateaus: Capitalism and schizophrenia.* (B. Massumi, Trans.). London: Aethlon.

Dodds, S. (2001). *Dance on screen: Genres and media from Hollywood to experimental art.* New York: Palgrave.

Elswit, K. (2012). *So You Think You Can Dance* does dance studies. TDR: *The Drama Review, 56*(1), 133–42.

Enli, G. S. (2009). Mass communication tapping into participatory culture: Exploring *Strictly Come Dancing* and *Britain's Got Talent. European Journal of Communication, 24,* 481–93.

Fisher, J., & Shay, A. (2009). *When men dance: Choreographing masculinities across borders.* New York: Oxford University Press.

Foster, S. (1996). The ballerina's Phallic pointe. In S. Foster (Ed.), *Corporealities: Dancing knowledge, culture and power* (1–25). London: Routledge.

Gard, M. (2008). *Men who dance: Aesthetics, athletics and art of masculinity.* New York: Peter Lang.

Greenaway, K. (2009, September 30). Dirty dancing: R-rated TV. *Edmonton Journal.*

Jordan, S., & Allen, D. (2003). *Parallel lines: Media representations of dance.* London: John Libbey.

Karthas, I. (2012). The politics of gender and the revival of ballet in early twentieth century France. *Journal of Social History, 45*(3), 960–69.

Lewis, N. (2008, October 8). Calgary can dance. *Calgary Herald,* C1.

Lorraine, T. (2008). Feminist lines of flight from the majoritarian subject. *Deleuze Studies, 2,* 60–82.

Market News Publishing. (2008, October 2). CTV Inc. *So You Think You Can Dance* reveals first-ever 20. Retrieved from http://www.newswire.ca/news-releases/so-you-think-you-can-dance-canada-reveals-first-ever-top-20-536668791.html

McMains, J. (2010). Reality check: *Dancing with the Stars* and the American dream. In J. Giersdorf, Y. Wong, & J. O'Shea (Eds.), *Routledge dance studies reader* (280–91). Florence, KY: Routledge.

Mitoma, J., Zimmer, E., & Stieber, D. A. (2002). *Envisioning dance on film and video.* London: Routledge.

Morris, G. (2005). Balanchine's bodies. *Body & Society, 11,* 19–44.

Quail, C. (2011). Nerds, geeks, and hip/square dialectic in contemporary television. *Television & New Media, 12,* 460–82.

Quinlan, M. M., & Bates, B. R. (2008). Dance and discourses of (dis)ability: Heather Mills's embodiment of disability on *Dancing with the Stars. Text and Performance Quarterly, 28*(1–2), 64–80.

Reason, M., & Reynolds, D. (2010). Special issue editorial: Screen dance audiences – Why now? *Participations, 7*(2). Retrieved from http://www.participations.org/Volume%207/Issue%202/PDF/introduction.pdf

Risner, D. (2009). *Stigma and perseverance in the lives of boys who dance: An empirical study of male identities in Western theatrical dance training.* Lewiston, NY: Edwin Mellen.

Sperounes, S. (2009, August 25). Edmonton dancer's dream kicks into overdrive. *Edmonton Journal,* B1.

Thomas, H. (2003). *The body, dance and cultural theory.* New York: Palgrave Macmillan.

Wulff, H. (1998). *Ballet across borders: Career and culture in the world of dancers.* New York: Berg.

Yeo, D. (2009, September 29). Dirty dancing, Canadian style. *Toronto Star.*

3

BALLET-INSPIRED WORKOUTS

Intersections of Ballet and Fitness

Pirkko Markula and Marianne I. Clark

As feminist scholars with an interest in the moving body, we have noted that contemporary culture is experiencing what might be called a dance moment. That is, dance appears to be creeping stealthily from the periphery of popular culture closer to the mainstream. Ballet in particular now intersects with glossy celebrity culture via women's fitness magazines that celebrate the sylphlike figures catapulted into the spotlight by the 2010 psycho-drama feature film *Black Swan* and espouse the aesthetic benefits of dance-inspired workouts. The slender ballerina and her pink satin pointe shoes seem to be captivating wider audiences than ever before.

As dancers and researchers, this emergent interest in ballet is surprising and encouraging to us. We are curious about the increasing intersections between ballet and women's fitness, yet wary of the implications of popular consumption of the idealized ballet body. Therefore, in this chapter we analyze ballet-inspired workouts as they appear online in popular women's magazines. To interrogate the intersections of ballet and fitness, we first review previous research that has analyzed the representations of the dancing body

and the fit, feminine body in the popular media. We then present
a feminist poststructuralist analysis of ballet-inspired workouts
that appear in six popular women's magazines—*Fitness, Health,
Prevention, Self, Shape,* and *Women's Health*—before commenting on
the wider consumption of the ballet body as an inspiration for the
fit, feminine body.

Dance and the Contemporary, Fit, Feminine Body Ideal

Previous dance research has suggested that the ballerina's body is
narrowly defined as young, extremely slim, sinewy, long, and lean,
and devoid of curves and extra flesh (Aalten, 2004; Foster, 1997;
Green, 1999, 2001; Ritenburg, 2010). Ritenburg (2010) argues that
this pervasive image of the exceedingly thin ballerina is widely
accepted and revered in the world of professional ballet, as well
as in mainstream popular culture. She analyzes photographs that
appear in promotional material of six principal dancers from the
New York City Ballet during the reign of choreographer George
Balanchine. All dancers were white, young, and very thin, "with
small breasts and narrow hips; their legs are long and lean; their
arms are long and slender; their torsos are short with a flat stom-
ach and abdomen; their heads are small atop a long, slender neck"
(Ritenburg, 2010, 75). Ritenburg argues that the idealization of this
homogenous extreme body type delegitimizes bodies of differing
shapes and sizes, as well as the aging, the disabled, and racialized
body within the world of ballet. She extended her project to include
articles that feature the female ballet body in popular magazines.
In the five articles she analyses, the female body was constructed as
a flawed object to be improved, and the ballet body was offered as
the idealized alternative. Ritenburg (2010) concludes that "in these
magazine articles, the discourse of the ballet dancer's body shape
is normalized as long and lean and with slim thighs...The ballet
dancer's body is understood as something to be desired and associated with specialized knowledge" (77).

Ritenburg's (2010) research underlines the persistence of the image of the long, lean, slender ballet body, and demonstrates the emerging intersections between dance and fitness. Although she does not provide further details of her sample or describe her analysis technique, her conclusions provide insight into the general messaging in popular magazines: the ballet body is constructed as desirable and attainable for the everyday woman. Her research also suggests that this version of the ballet body is becoming consumed more widely in popular culture. Although there is scant research analyzing the ballet body in popular media, there is a substantial body of literature on the representations of the fit, feminine body in the media.

The fit, feminine body has long been of interest to feminist scholars (Duncan, 1994; Dworkin & Wachs, 2009; Jette, 2006; Lloyd, 1996; Markula, 1995, 2001; Markula & Kennedy, 2011; Maguire, 2007), who, from various theoretical perspectives, have indicated that "media images of the fit body align closely with the singular ideal, thin, toned and youthful looking feminine body" (Markula & Kennedy, 2011, 4). This fit body should not be too muscular, but toning certain "problem spots," such as hips, thighs, butt, abdominals, and underarms, with constant exercise can lead to the proper lean and sexy look (Dworkin & Wachs, 2009; Markula, 1995).

The idealized notion of good looks has become closely intertwined with health in the popular fitness media texts that now celebrate the thin and toned body as the healthy body. Therefore, achieving the idealized fit body is constructed as desirable and benign in the name of health (Dworkin & Wachs, 2009; Jette, 2006; Markula, 2001; McGannon & Spence, 2012). Dworkin and Wachs (2009) argue that this connection reinforces neoliberal notions of individual responsibility for health: "Over time, individual involvement becomes self-improvement and the neoliberal marketplace becomes an imperative part of the construction of the healthy self" (172–73). Several researchers from various theoretical perspectives have confirmed that the responsibility for attaining the healthy-looking body is assigned to individual women (Duncan, 1994;

Markula, 2001; Maguire, 2007) in a consumerist culture that produces feminine subjects in need of "fixing" through specific bodily practices and fitness-related products and services (McGannon & Spence, 2012; Kennedy & Pappa, 2011; Mansfield, 2011).

Several feminist Foucauldian scholars (Duncan, 1994; Eskes, Duncan, & Miller, 1998; Jette, 2006; Lloyd, 1996; Markula, 2001; Markula & Kennedy, 2011; Markula & Pringle, 2006; McGannon & Spence, 2012) have exposed the power mechanics that sustain the widespread promotion and celebration of the idealized, healthy-looking feminine body. They observe that such a body shape has been promoted as "normal" in Western cultures and, as a result, women learn to demonstrate commitment to the ideal body. Consequently, women engage in disciplined exercise routines, stringent body monitoring, and self-surveillance to achieve the desired, normal body. The normalization of the fit ideal body and the practices necessary to produce that body are supported by a set of discourses, or knowledges (Markula, 2014), that often go unexamined and evade critique. We return to define fitness discourses more closely in our methodology section.

In summary, feminist researchers locate women's fitness within consumer culture where an idealized, desirable feminine body has turned to connote the healthy body (Markula & Kennedy, 2011). As a result, women's fitness has become a tool for perpetuating and maintaining salient narratives that reproduce narrowly defined ideals of white, heterosexual, middle-class femininity (Dworkin & Wachs, 2009; Kennedy & Markula, 2011; McGannon & Spence, 2012; Maguire, 2007) through disciplined body work and self-surveillance. The ballet-inspired fitness workouts have now emerged in this consumerist environment. Therefore, in this chapter we ask, what type of body is constructed and reproduced through ballet-inspired workouts? What fitness practices are promoted in these workouts? How are the idealized body shape and ballet-inspired fitness practices sustained within the consumer culture? To address these questions, we perform a Foucauldian analysis of both the written text and visuals presented in online workout articles in popular women's magazines.

Methodology

This chapter elaborates on existing studies of ballet and exercise in the popular media by drawing upon Deleuze's (1988) work on Foucault's (1976) "discursive formation." This formation refers to the set of rules and conditions that allow for the production and intelligibility of certain identifiable knowledges, such as "fitness" or "dance." We locate the ballet-inspired barre workouts within the discursive formation (Foucault, 1976) of fitness. In this formation, certain relations are maintained through the tactical use of articulable discourses and visible non-discursive elements within the online ballet-based workouts. Examples of articulable discourses may include physiology, psychology, medicine, and cultural notions of the aesthetics of the healthy-looking body. Visible non-discursive elements refer to the physical practices and bodies that appear in the workouts. A discursive formation, thus, is made up of both visible forms and articulable forms. As Deleuze (1988) emphasizes, "Knowledge...is defined by the combinations of visible and articulable...Knowledge is practical assemblage, a 'mechanism' of statements and visibilities" (44). Deleuze further defines power as an exercise of force, and knowledge as a regulation of these force relations. Following Deleuze, we analyze both the articulable and visible knowledges in our sample of online ballet-based workouts to determine how these texts might regulate or be regulated by the existing force relations supporting the current discursive formation of women's fitness.

Sample

For this project, we utilized a criterion-based sampling strategy (Patton, 2002). We selected texts for analysis by identifying workouts that were (a) explicitly ballet-inspired (indicated by the headline text); (b) included more than one exercise performed at or with the barre; and (c) contained both written text (articulable) and photographic (visible) components.

In addition, we focused on online workouts appearing on women's magazine websites as these websites have a broader reach than print distribution. We limited our sample to articles published between 2010 and 2015 as we considered this time frame to be inclusive and reflective of the most recent fitness trends. We included only popular magazine titles, such as *Shape*, *Women's Health*, and *Prevention*, as we wanted to capture workouts targeted to a general, female audience. The following combinations of search terms were used: "dance workouts," "barre," "ballet," "fitness magazine," "women's workouts," "dance," "magazines," "barre workouts," and "women's fitness." We entered three search terms at a time and reviewed the first twenty hits from each search as these were the most visible and accessible articles for those searching for online workouts. From these searches, ten articles from six magazines met these criteria (see Appendix A).

Analysis of the Visible

Deleuze (1988) characterizes the visible aspects of a discursive formation as "an assembly of organs and functions that makes something visible" (59–60). In the context of the online ballet-inspired workouts, the visible aspects are the images of the bodies that demonstrate the workout, the equipment they used, and the space (e.g., a studio) where they were pictured.[1] Consequently, our analysis included a detailed description of the model (clothing, facial expression) who demonstrated each workout—all ten workouts displayed one model demonstrating each exercise—and equipment used (e.g., barre, chair, weights, gliders). We did not include a detailed description of the space because the model was the dominant image, whereas the space was limited to depictions of parts of the floor, walls (where the barre was attached), and, occasionally, a mirror.

Deleuze (1988) further emphasizes that the visibilities are "not defined by sight but are complexes of actions and passions, actions and reactions, multisensorial complexes, which emerge into the light of day" (50). Therefore, it was important to include an analysis of exercise practices as a part of the visible formations. In our analysis, we recorded each exercise in detail using either the French dance vocabulary or, if not suitable, an anatomical description of the movement. In addition, we recorded the muscles involved in the exercise to determine links between the articulable knowledges and visible exercise practice. For example, by recording the muscle work we could identify whether the ballet-inspired workouts targeted the problem areas of the fit, ideal body or whether they provided possible alternative ways of understanding exercise with their intersections of ballet. The visible information from the sample was recorded in a table form for further careful comparison with the articulable (see Appendix B).

Analysis of the Articulable

One of Foucault's (1978) major concepts, discourse, provides a basis for an analysis of the articulable form of knowledge. In Foucault's (1978) work, the term *discourse* assumes multiple meanings, but he asserted that "discourses are tactical elements or blocks operating in the field of force relations, [sic] there can exist different and even contradictory discourses within the same strategy; they can, on the contrary, circulate without changing their form from one strategy to another, opposing strategy" (101–02). In terms of women's exercise, articulable information would consist of how exercise is talked about—articulated—in, for example, the popular media texts. Previous research on women's exercise has identified several ways to articulate women's fitness such as the aesthetics of the ideal, healthy-looking body, and the medical, exercise science research on disease prevention (e.g., Markula & Kennedy, 2011). We continued this analysis of the articulable discourses by examining the text appearing in the workouts (e.g., the descriptions of the exercises). A Foucauldian textual analysis allowed us to identify whether the ways the ballet-inspired workouts were described or articulated aligned with the current dominant exercise discourses, or whether they used other forms of knowledge as their support. The intent was not to label a particular discourse as good or bad, liberating or oppressive, but rather to explore what discourses were present.

Foucault (1976) proposes an analysis for identifying various concepts, statements, and theories available in specific texts. Following his lead, we first examined the concepts—the various discursive elements that can be linked together to create comprehensible ways to talk about a specific object—in the ballet-inspired workout texts. The following concepts emerged through our careful reading: body parts and muscles, bodily action, dance-specific movement, body aesthetics, and fitness. Many concepts overlapped between articles due to their shared purpose (to provide instruction for a ballet-inspired workout) and content (i.e., description of each exercise). These concepts were then organized into individualized groups of statements that linked the concepts together to reflect a particular, coherent way of talking about fitness. We identified twelve statements that linked each of the concepts together (see Appendix C). At this stage, we asked how the individual statements linked with a larger field of statements (Markula & Silk, 2011): the theoretical formations. We were then able to identify how various articulable elements produced theories about ballet-inspired workouts and the fit, feminine body throughout the texts. Our analysis resulted in three main theories: ballet-inspired workouts are an efficient way to a lean and sculpted body; dance exercises need to be combined with fitness exercises; and ballet-inspired workouts are workouts for every woman. Finally, an important step for Foucauldian analysis is to connect the theories to larger knowledges or discourses and then to power relations. In this stage, we asked, what are the dominant understandings and meanings of the fit, ballet body that emerge throughout these workouts? What power relations have enabled this particular understanding of this body to become dominant?

Results

As a general structure, the ten ballet-inspired workouts included opening paragraphs that briefly introduced the workout, provided a rationale for its ballet inspiration, and emphasized the benefits of the exercises. There were two main rationales: first, to achieve the desirable aesthetics of a dancer's body, which was described as sculpted, lean, and toned; and second, to achieve this body fast. These routines claimed to produce quick results, but didn't explain how such results would come about so quickly. For example, *Self* magazine assured readers that they would "see results faster," and *Shape* magazine urged the readers to "sculpt a lean dancer's body on your own schedule." The articles then continued to provide specific directions for each of the exercises (five to ten per workout). Still photographs illustrated the verbal descriptions. One article, "Barre Moves that You Can Do at Home," provided moving images that made it easy to follow the movement pattern of each exercise.

In our discussion, we have combined the analysis of the articulable component (the text) of each workout with an analysis of the visible component (the photographs) to illustrate the discursive formation within which the ballet-inspired workouts were located. We have further organized this section based on the three theories that emerged through the analysis of the concepts and the statements linking the concepts.

Efficient Way to a Lean and Sculpted Body

The article texts promise that engaging in ballet-inspired workouts is a more efficient and expedient way for exercising women to achieve a lean, sculpted body than conventional workouts. This theory had two components. The first referred to the action of reshaping and changing general body size and shape. The second captured more specific movement performed by individual body parts. This theory, however, supported the specific body aesthetics that appeared in all of the articles: the appearance of the fit, dancing body that was assured as an outcome if the workout were performed regularly. A body that appeared slim, toned, lean, and sculpted was described similarly in all texts as the idealized, fit, dancing body (see also Ritenburg, 2010). Interestingly, however, only one of the women demonstrating the workouts appeared to exemplify the stereotypical young and thin aesthetic of a (non-exerciser) model, whereas the others were more mature program designers or dancers (but not necessarily identified as ballerinas). We expand this discussion in connection to the third theory below.

The sculpted body also reflected dominant understandings in women's fitness magazines about so-called problem areas (Dworkin & Wachs, 2009; Markula, 1995; Markula & Kennedy, 2011) that needed to be improved through exercise; the thighs, hips, butt, and waist were frequently identified as targets for improvement. Although the ballet-based workouts involved weights, they were light weights that worked to build the appropriate tone for the ideal feminine body instead of heavy weights for "muscle bulk" (Dworkin & Wachs, 2009). These exercises targeted the upper body to train the superficial shoulder muscle, deltoid, and the arm muscles— biceps and triceps brachii. While the floor workouts included only a few exercises for hip abductors and adductors—commonly identified as the "problems spots" of women's bodies—they aligned with the previous feminist researchers' findings of exercise target-ing isolated body parts (Markula, 1995). These so-called problem body parts were also identified as the ones where women would notice results if they engaged in the dance workout. For example, the workout, "Want a Dancer's Body?" in *Prevention* promised to "strengthen your deepest belly muscles...while lifting your butt, trimming your thighs, and toning your arms."

In the detailed descriptions of each exercise, both body parts (e.g., thighs) and specific muscles (e.g., "glutes") were named. When referred to as a target for improvement, the names of body parts, not muscles, were used most often. For example, in a *Fitness* maga-zine workout titled "5 Beginner Barre Exercises You Can Do at Home," all the exercises promised to improve the hips, butt, thighs, and legs. Many of the workouts included heavy use of relevé (raising up to one's toes), which added significant work for calf muscles, yet larger or more toned calves were not included in the list of improved body parts. Similarly, because turn-out was commonly involved, the rotator muscles enabling this movement were heavily loaded, yet were never mentioned as a target muscle group in the exercise descriptions.

In addition, the ballet-inspired workouts instructed the exercising women to move in particular ways to participate in the workout. These ways of moving involved general body parts (e.g., arms, legs), and the exercise motions were described in detailed bodily action. For example, waists were to be "whittled" and readers were told to "extend," "pull," or "flex" certain body parts to execute the exercise. The "Burn Fat with Ballet" workout in *Health* magazine instructed readers to "Extend left leg diagonally back with toes pointed...lift and lower leg a couple of inches." The workouts also instructed readers to perform a specific number of repetitions of each exercise and to repeat them on each side of the body. Foucault (1976) understands this numerical organization of exercise as a technique of discipline. The prescribed number of repetitions, therefore, contribute to the disciplinary aspect of the ballet-inspired workouts.

Dance Exercises Need to Be Combined with Fitness Exercise

As indicated by their label, all the ballet-inspired workouts combined ballet exercises at the barre with traditional fitness exercises, often performed on the floor, and cardiovascular activity. This combination was to result in physical fitness and build the fit, feminine body. The texts indicated, first, that workouts with a warm-up, cool-down, and cardiovascular exertion would result in physical fitness, and, second, that conventional fitness exercises such as "lunges," "rows," and "curls" were necessary for building a fit body. Some of the names reflected controversial exercise practices that are now deemed unsuitable or even unhealthy (e.g., parallel quad burner). In the workout "5 Barre Moves You Can Do At Home" in

Self magazine, readers were instructed to challenge themselves with a slight modification "to intensify the burn in the hammies."

It must be noted that there were no visuals related to cardiovascular fitness activities. A significant portion of the pictured exercises (twenty-eight out of fifty-nine exercises), however, were what we identified above as conventional fitness exercises. As many of these were performed either standing, sitting, or lying on the floor and/or using weights (rather than the barre), we call them floor exercises. A typical ballet class, although it includes some movement combinations performed at the centre of the studio, does not include floor exercises. Many of the floor exercises pictured in the ballet-inspired workouts—different forms of sit-ups (eight exercises), lunges (eight exercises), and arm exercises with free weights (twelve exercises)—could be included in any fitness workout. In this sense, they did not provide new, alternative, or different ways of moving even if now labelled with a ballet-inspired name (e.g., lower abs attitude, arabesque push-up, plié port de bras, dancer's twist).

Although all the workouts in our sample were considered barre workouts, only thirty-three of fifty-nine exercises used a ballet barre, or an equivalent support such as a chair. These barre exercises conveyed more of a connection to dance than the floor exercises. They, distinct from fitness, were referred to by ballet-specific names such as relevé passé, grand plié, arabesque attitude, reaching ronde de jambe, grand battement, dégagé, which are used in teaching ballet repertoire. The dance-related movements also referred to aesthetic movement qualities—elegant, graceful, and having good posture—to describe dancers. *Prevention* claimed that the workout it provided would help readers obtain the "graceful, sculpted body of a dancer" and "whip into shape your perfect-posture muscles." These qualities were commonly celebrated in the introductory paragraphs and represented as attainable for exercising women through adherence to the dance-inspired workout. Therefore, dance-related statements reflected dominant ideas about the appearance of dancing bodies *and* their movement quality—namely, gracefulness.

The most visible ballet-like characteristic was the "turn-out" of the legs; twenty of thirty-three barre exercises were performed in turn-out. The accompanying texts often told the exercisers to position their feet with heels together and toes pointed outward (known as "first position" in ballet) to describe the turn-out.

The most common barre exercises were pliés (bending and then straightening both knees) in first (seven exercises) and second (ten exercises) ballet position. These were often combined with relevé (heels lifted, feet in demi-pointe position). High leg extensions to the back— arabesques/attitudes (thirteen exercises)—and forward— battements, dégagés (five exercises)—were also frequently included as barre exercises.

Because these exercises were performed standing up, they explicitly targeted the leg muscles and were obviously designed to shape the exercisers' legs into the lean and long ballet look. Indeed, one workout explained that all its barre exercises were intended for "the hip, butt, thighs, legs." In this sense, they were not seen as isolating a particular muscle group similar to the floor exercises but nevertheless continued to focus on the familiar lower body problem spots (Dworkin & Wachs, 2009; Markula, 1995).

Workouts for Every Woman

The texts in online ballet-inspired workouts indicated that the exercises were designed to be performed anywhere and did not require the availability of a studio or previous knowledge of dance repertoire. Therefore, they could be performed efficiently and easily by women without dance training. In these texts, the exercising women were categorized as dancers strictly based on appearance (sculpted, good posture, long legs). Bodies that complied with these criteria could be understood as "dancer bodies." Consequently, bodies that did not comply were non-dancing bodies. Notably, dancing bodies did not have to exhibit dance skill. The visual representation, nevertheless, displayed models with various backgrounds.

All the models were women, but differed in their ability to demonstrate ballet movement. In the strictest sense, they were not the uniformly young, toned, and very thin models common in popular exercise media (Dworkin & Wachs, 2009). One workout was inspired by "sexy star" Allison Williams, who did not demonstrate the exercises. While all the demonstrating models wore tight, skin-hugging exercise clothes, there were also more mature-looking models, several of whom were instructors or program designers, and thus could be assumed to have a significant ballet background.

A thin-looking body did not assure the quality of movement that the texts called for. One workout, "The Best and Worst Barre Exercises," featured a young woman who was so obviously a non-dancer that even the reader comments on the web page pointed to her inexperience. She was, however, probably the closest to an average exerciser who is unfamiliar with the arm positioning or leg turn-out in barre classes. This workout also elicited readers to comment on the justifications that characterized some exercises as "bad." Based on our dance backgrounds, we agreed that an attitude (back) or plié relevé in second position are demanding for exercisers without the necessary technical training, but were also surprised to learn that grand battement—one of the most demanding ballet exercises—was deemed a safe exercise. It was, perhaps, unsurprising that exercises considered "the best" were all performed in parallel position instead of in turn-out, and also closely resembled movements included in other types of fitness workouts (squat to lunge, leg lift back, squat with calf raise). Based on this assessment, the ballet movements—the movements that distinguish the barre workouts from other types of workouts—are, in fact, the exercises to avoid. This article, then, works to erase the differences between a barre workout and other exercise routines while, no doubt, providing much needed caution for non-dancers who want to attempt ballet exercises.

Four of the workouts were demonstrated either by owners of studios that offer barre workouts (Julie Erickson, Kristine Storie) or by women who have designed barre workout programs for fitness industry franchises (Kara Liotta, FlyBarre; Kristine Storie, Xtend Barre; Michelle Demus Auerbach, BFX studio barre program creator). Comparisons between these professionals revealed an emphasis on a particular movement quality resulting from different training backgrounds. Of these four relatively mature and experienced fitness professionals, only Auerbach appeared to have a dance background. Her sharply pointed feet, extended legs, arm positioning, and general poise (with lifted core, lowered shoulder blades, and long neck) positioned her as a dancer. Her movement vocabulary also included some exercises requiring the use of multiple body parts at several planes instead of exercises targeting only isolated body parts and provided some innovation that expanded the typical exercise workout mode. Many of Auerbach's exercises also required a large range of motion, particularly at the hip joint, and deep knee bends in positions not usually performed in everyday life. Performed by her, they looked easy and graceful but were nevertheless demanding movements that might be contraindicated for an exerciser without a dance background.

Erickson, who offered five beginner barre exercises (four at the barre and one floor exercise known as "pretzel"), was the only one who referred to dance quality in her verbal instructions, directing the readers to "create a long line from heels to crown" or to "recheck" their "posture" ("5 Beginner Barre Exercises"). Although Erickson appeared to lack the dance poise of Auerbach, she attempted a very high arabesque/attitude position in (semi) turn-out and standing leg in (low) relevé. This is a demanding exercise that did not seem suitable for a beginner who would be attempting the workout at home. Liotta and Storie demonstrated a workout where Storie provided the floor exercises—which had no dance-specific component—and Liotta the barre exercises. These two barre exercises, passé press and back attitude and tendu lift, required turn-out and arm positioning from dance training. Liotta's movement, however, revealed elementary technical deficiencies such as a "sickled foot" that in ballet can result in dangerous, injury-prone movement practices. She did not exhibit the poise and arm positioning of a dancer. Considering that these three women were program developers and barre-specific studio owners, the level of actual dance training required to create successful ballet-inspired workouts seemed low. Unlike Ritenburg (2010), we did not find ballet "associated with specialized knowledge" (77) in these online workout texts.

Based on our analysis, the online ballet-inspired workouts can be divided into familiar floor exercises, which were renamed or modified slightly for ballet-inspired workouts, and the barre exercises, which provided the connection to ballet. When demonstrated by models with dance backgrounds, the barre exercises, while appearing effortless and graceful, were very difficult and potentially injury-inducing (e.g., deep second position plié) for an average exerciser at home. When demonstrated by models without a dance background, the exercises lost their dance quality. Probably the most dangerous exercises were the technically demanding ballet exercises (arabesque/attitude) when demonstrated poorly. This presents an interesting dilemma: if ballet exercises that require technical training are potentially too dangerous, must they be modified to more closely resemble traditional exercise vocabulary (e.g., performed in parallel), or changed to more commonly used exercises (e.g., lunge)? What is the role of ballet-inspired workouts in women's online health and fitness magazines?

Dance Aesthetics for the Fit, Lean Body

In this chapter, we examined what type of body (and through what fitness practices) was promoted in ballet-inspired workouts through textual articulation and visual presentation. We concluded that through these texts, ballet and fitness were combined into workouts that promised to help women efficiently attain the desirable feminine body. These texts also prescribed discursive practices that were positioned as a means to achieve the idealized fit, sculpted, lean body. The exercises were designed to target the familiar problem spots in women's bodies: belly, bums, and thighs. In this sense, the workouts did not add to the existing dimensions of women's exercise regimes identified by previous feminist researchers. If anything, the articulable elements seemed to tighten the requirements for the fit-looking body by adding features of the ballet body such as "lean legs" (Ritenburg, 2010) to the fitness vocabulary.

In addition, these magazine workouts were advertised as easy exercises for the readers to do at home. It is important to keep in mind that ballet exercises were originally designed to improve a ballerina's performance, and thus are meant to develop a dancer's technical ability. If re-assigned purely as "body-shapers" without the detailed emphasis of learning ballet technique, they easily turn dysfunctional. For example, the ballet-inspired barre exercises were to result in "lean legs," although they could have potentially strengthened a variety of muscle groups (calf muscles, deep rotators, iliopsoas, gluteus maximus, quadriceps, and hamstrings) if performed with adequate technical proficiency. However, an average exerciser does not immediately possess the range of motion in the hips or the dancer's co-ordination to sustain the core and upper body alignment while also performing demanding leg extensions. While the text offers some safety precautions, such as "turn legs out from hip sockets only" ("5 Beginner Barre Exercises"), the visuals tend to focus on the maximum range of motion in pliés and extreme extensions in arabesques. These movements are impossible without instructions on how to perform the correct technique and/or modifications leading to the performance of proper turn-out, for example. The visual presentation seems to imply that each exercise could be performed, to its maximum immediately; as long as the exerciser "embrace[d] one's inner ballerina," it was possible to achieve "a dancer's body."

To understand the cultural meaning of the ballet-inspired workouts, we now locate our articulable and visible elements within the larger discursive formation (Deleuze, 1988; Foucault, 1976) of fitness. We identify connections to the dominant discourses of women's exercise and dance to assess how these workouts were shaped by these broader understandings of women's physical activity. While the visible elements have attracted less interest, previous feminist research (Markula & Kennedy, 2011) has identified that knowledges (or discourses) such as physiology, medicine, psychology, and aesthetics of the healthy-looking body are tactically used to maintain the current consumerist fitness field in neoliberal societies. Ritenburg (2010) similarly recognizes that the images of the perfect ballet body in popular dance magazines and even children's books maintain dominant understandings of ballet and femininity. Based on our analysis, the three articulable theories (barre workouts are efficient ways to a lean and sculpted body; dance exercises in barre workouts need to be combined with fitness exercise; barre workouts are workouts for every woman) can all be linked to the social discourse of the aesthetics of the fit, feminine body. The connection to ballet was limited to references of the perfect ballet body that then amplified the focus on body shaping. The articulable and visible elements connected to ballet (e.g., names of the exercises, use of dancers as models, dance-specific exercises, the barre) serve as means for the narrowly defined thin, toned, sculpted, fit, perfect, feminine body. Although grace, balance, and the unique qualities of the dancing body were mentioned frequently in introductory paragraphs or sub-headlines, they were not mentioned in the exercise descriptions. There was no reference to expressiveness or dance skill. When demonstrated by untrained models, the visible movement images further downplayed the aspects of dance quality. Therefore, the technical dimension, bodily experience, or expression—all important components of dance—were replaced by conventional workout routines that served as efficient tools to obtain the idealized fit, feminine body. The connection to the ballet body further narrowed the parameters of the fit-looking body.

The floor exercises that are absent in ballet training connected the ballet-inspired workouts with fitness. While the text emphasized the main components of physical fitness (cardiovascular, body composition, muscle strength, and endurance) by recommending the traditional structure of warm-up, exercise session, and cooldown, health—physical or psychological—was never mentioned.

Consequently, the exercises were not designed for illness prevention, improved psychological health, or everyday functionality.
Notably, flexibility, usually considered the trademark of a ballerina
(Foster, 1997; Aalten, 2004), was only explicitly mentioned in the
introductory paragraphs of two articles. It was not discussed in the
corresponding exercise instructions, nor were flexibility-specific
exercises (stretches) pictured as visual images. As the workouts
were devoid of the original purpose of ballet training (professional
technical ability), they almost exclusively focused on changing
exercisers' appearance, and suggested that women's physical fitness
can be determined through bodily appearance. Dominated by the
idea of bodily appearance, the ballet-inspired workouts did not
introduce any novel articulable or visible forms to the discursive
formation of women's fitness.

Conclusion

Our analysis indicated that the ballet-inspired workouts did not
offer substantially new ways of knowing about fitness or the
fit body. The ballet connection did, however, result in a use of
"experts," such as program designers and studio owners, to provide
specialized dance knowledge. Foucault (1978) locates such experts
within the disciplinary, confessional framework where individuals are to trust and then follow expert advice instead of engaging
in critical evaluation of such practices themselves. In the ballet-
inspired workouts, these experts were often more mature women
who do not usually appear in magazine workouts. Their expertise
was largely established by their studio ownership or status within
a particular studio, not by their educational backgrounds or dance
teaching experience. While all of them, no doubt, had significant
fitness industry experience, they, unlike in Ritenburg's (2010) study
of ballet in popular magazines, did not necessarily demonstrate
extensive dance background. The ballet-inspired workouts, thus,

turned either into "normal" workouts with poorly demonstrated dance moves or well-executed but demanding movements for someone without the appropriate dance skill.

In consumerist fitness culture, narrowly defined body aesthetics continue to be the major selling point of the ballet-inspired workouts; the connection to ballet, with its even more strictly defined body ideal of being extremely thin and lean without bulky muscles, provides yet a tougher challenge for the exercising woman. At the same time, the qualities of dance movement (e.g., grace), posture, and the pose of a confident dancing body can appeal to many women. These qualities, however, are difficult to obtain without previous dance training and technique. They were, therefore, not as central or as important as body aesthetics in these online workouts.

We conclude, therefore, that the online ballet-inspired workouts are deployed strategically in contemporary fitness magazines to reproduce dominant understandings of the fit, feminine body, and to encourage women to take responsibility for building such a body by engaging in specific practices. For example, in the introductory paragraphs, the efficiency of the workouts and the ease with which they could be performed, without special equipment, space, or skill requirements, were emphasized, which results in a sense that there was little excuse for women not to engage in these fitness practices, anywhere, any time. Indeed, *Women's Health* described its feature workout as "excuse proof." Consequently, like previous feminist Foucauldian exercise researchers (Duncan, 1994; Eskes et al., 1998; Jette, 2006; Markula, 2001; McDermott, 2011) have argued, women readers were assigned individual responsibility, typical in neoliberal society, to engage in the workouts in order to achieve the lean and sculpted body that was celebrated as attainable if only they worked hard enough. Additionally, the articles normalized ballet-inspired workouts with statements such as "women everywhere are flocking to barre workout classes" ("Embrace Your Inner Ballerina") and "everywhere you look folks are bellying up the barre" ("Burn Fat with Ballet").

In conclusion, ballet-inspired workouts can act as disciplinary practices that, supported by specific articulable discourses, become normal (Foucault, 1991). When located within the discursive formation of fitness, the articulable and visible elements of online ballet-inspired workouts tactically maintain the existing consumerist promotion of the narrowly defined fit, feminine body. In addition, it is individual women's responsibility to engage in body sculpting in a neoliberal society where, as Deleuze (1988) emphasizes, knowledge regulates how the force of power is directed. The existing force relations continue to steer the current discursive formation of fitness-based knowledge toward thin and toned feminine bodies.

Note

1. Deleuze (1988) adds that distribution of space, ordering of time, and composition of space-time should be considered when discussing the visible aspects. Foucault (1991) labels these "values" as disciplinary techniques designed to produce "docile bodies." Such docile bodies are continually transformed and improved to become "useful," productive, but controlled citizens. Some previous work has analyzed how the locations of exercise (or the visible form) create docility (Markula & Pringle, 2006).

References

Aalten, A. (2004). "The moment when it all comes together": Embodied experiences in ballet. *European Journal of Women's Studies, 11*(3), 263–76. doi: 10.1177/1350506804044462

Deleuze, G. (1988). *Foucault.* (S. Head, Trans.). London: Athlone.

Duncan, M. C. (1994). The politics of women's body image and practices: Foucault, the Panopticon and *Shape* magazine. *Journal of Sport and Social Issues, 18,* 48–65.

Dworkin, S. L., & Wachs, F. L. (2009). *Body panic: Gender, health and the selling of fitness.* New York: New York University Press.

Eskes, T. B., Duncan, M. C., & Miller. E. M. (1998). The discourse of empowerment: Foucault, Marcuse, and women's fitness texts. *Journal of Sport and Social Issues, 22,* 317–44.

Foster, S. L. (1997). Dancing bodies. In J. C. Desmond (Ed.), *Meaning in motion: New cultural studies in dance* (235–58). Durham, NC: Duke University Press.

Foucault, M. (1976). *The archaeology of knowledge and the discourse on language.* (A. M. Sheridan Smith, Trans.). New York: Pantheon Books.

Foucault, M. (1978). *History of sexuality. Volume 1: An introduction.* (R. Hurley, Trans.). London: Penguin Books.

Foucault, M. (1991). *Discipline and punish: The birth of the prison* (A. Sheridan, Trans.). London: Penguin Books.

Green, J. (1999). Somatic authority and the myth of the ideal body in dance education. *Dance Research Journal, 31*(2), 80–100.

Green, J. (2001). Socially constructed bodies in American dance classrooms. *Research in Dance Education, 2,* 155–72.

Jette, S. (2006). Fit for two? A critical discourse analysis of *Oxygen* fitness magazine. *Sociology of Sport Journal, 23,* 331–51.

Kennedy, E., & Markula, P. (2011). *Women and exercise: The body, health and consumerism.* New York: Routledge.

Kennedy, E., & Pappa, E. (2011). Love your body? The discursive construction of exercising women's lifestyle and fitness magazines. In E. Kennedy & P. Markula (Eds.), *Women and exercise: The body, health and consumerism* (29–43). New York: Routledge.

Lloyd, M. (1996). Feminism, aerobics and the politics of the body. *Body & Society, 2*(2), 79–98.

Maguire, J. S. (2007). *Fit for consumption: Sociology and the business of fitness.* London: Routledge.

Mansfield, L. (2011). Fit, fat and feminine? The stigmatization of fat women in fitness gyms. In E. Kennedy & P. Markula (Eds.), *Women and exercise: The body, health and consumerism* (81–100). New York: Routledge.

Markula, P. (1995). Firm but shapely, fit but sexy, strong but thin: The postmodern aerobicizing female bodies. *Sociology of Sport Journal, 12,* 424–53.

Markula, P. (2001). Beyond the perfect body: Women's body image distortion in fitness magazine discourse. *Journal of Sport & Social Issues, 25,* 158–79.

Markula, P. (2014). The moving body and social change. *Cultural Studies – Critical Methodologies, 14,* 471–82. doi:10.1177/1532708614541892

Markula, P., & Kennedy, E. (2011). Introduction. Beyond binaries: Contemporary approaches to women and exercise. In E. Kennedy & P. Markula (Eds.), *Women and exercise: The body, health and consumerism* (1–26). New York: Routledge.

Markula, P., & Pringle, R. (2006). *Foucault, sport and exercise: Power, knowledge and transforming the self.* New York: Routledge.

Markula, P., & Silk, M. (2011). *Qualitative research for physical culture.* Basingstoke, UK: Palgrave.

McDermott, L. (2011). "Doing something that's good for me": Exploring intersections of physical activity and health. In E. Kennedy and P. Markula (Eds.), *Women and exercise: The body, health and consumerism* (197–226). New York: Routledge.

McGannon, K. R., & Spence, J. C. (2012). Exploring news media representations of women's exercise and subjectivity through critical discourse analysis. *Qualitative Research in Sport, Exercise and Health, 4*, 32–50.

Patton, M. (2002). *Qualitative research and evaluation methods.* Thousand Oaks, CA: Sage.

Ritenburg, H. D. (2010). Frozen landscapes: A Foucauldian genealogy of the ideal ballet dancer's body. *Research in Dance Education, 11*, 71–85.

Appendix A

Magazine Articles Included in Analysis

Aldridge, K. (2014, December 5). Allison William's core fusion barre workout. *Shape*. Retrieved April 16, 2015, from http://www.shape.com/celebrities/celebrity-workouts/allison-williams-core-fusion-barre-workout

Angle. S. (2013, November 27). 5 barre moves you can do at home. *Self*. Retrieved April 16, 2015, from http://www.self.com/story/five-barre-moves-you-can-do-at-home

Ator, J. (2010, January 10). Sculpt a lean body. *Women's Health*. Retrieved April 15, 2015, http://www.womenshealthmag.com/fitness/isometric-exercises

Matthews, J. (n.d.). The best and worst barre exercises. *Shape*. Retrieved April 16, 2015, http://www.shape.com/fitness/workouts/best-and-worst-barre-exercises

Reid-St. John, S. (n.d.). Burn fat with ballet. *Health*. Retrieved April 15, 2015, http://www.health.com/health/gallery/0,,20532644,00.html

Self Staff. (2014, November 17). Firm fast with 6 simple ballet-inspired moves. *Self*. Retrieved April 15, 2015, http://www.self.com/gallery/firm-fast-simple-ballet-moves-slideshow

Smith, J. (n.d.). Home barre workout: Ballet belly, buns and thighs. *Shape*. Retrieved April 15, 2015, from http://www.shape.com/fitness/workouts/home-barre-workout-ballet-belly-buns-and-thighs

Smith, J. (n.d.) At-home barre workout: Embrace your inner ballerina. *Shape*. Retrieved April 15, 2015, http://www.shape.com/fitness/workouts/home-barre-workout

Southerland, J.B. (2012, March 5). Want a dancer's body? *Prevention*. Retrieved April 16, 2015, http://www.prevention.com/fitness/strength-training/ballet-boot-camp-barre-fitness

Travers, C. (n.d.). 5 beginner barre exercises you can do home. *Fitness*. Retrieved April 15, 2015, http://www.fitnessmagazine.com/workout/pilates/exercises/beginner-barre-exercises/

Appendix B

Example of Analysis of Raw Visible Data

This really was quite a nice workout and the model was good—however, this routine could be very demanding for an average exerciser, the grand plié side crunch in particular. The model has good extensions and is shown wearing ankle-length black tights and long, sleeveless, pink top. This exercise comes from *Shape* magazine, "Home Barre Workout: Ballet Belly, Buns and Thighs," by Jessica Smith.

Movement	Barre	Muscle(s)
Relevé passé rotation From parallel first to passé with upper body rotation	Chair	• Calf muscles • Psoas • Latissimus dorsi
Grand plié side crunch Second plié, turn-out side bend to attitude to side	Chair	• Rotators • Adductors • Psoas • Latissimus dorsi
Elevated plank Leaning on the chair, arabesque parallel to knee lift front	Chair	• Gluteus maximus • Abdominals • Psoas
Lower abs attitude Sitting, leaning back on elbows, legs lifted, turned out – lower legs to floor	Floor	• Abdominals
Arabesque push-up Upper body lowered in push-up, rest of the body on the side, upper leg extended Bend upper leg, push arms straight	Floor	• Abductors • Triceps

Appendix C

Analysis of the Articulable Statements that Linked the Concepts Together

- Ballet dancers have desirable lean, sculpted bodies, which are attainable through ballet-based workouts.
- Ballet dancers are graceful, flexible, and have good posture.
- Performing ballet-based workouts will help women obtain the sculpted ballet body quickly.
- Ballet-based workouts target multiple muscles and body parts that are often viewed as problem areas on women (e.g., butt, thighs).
- Performing ballet-based workouts requires body parts and muscles to move in specific ways.
- The ballet-based workout is accessible to any woman; no special space, equipment or training is required.
- Engaging in ballet-based workouts will produce a slim, toned body that is also graceful.
- Ballet has a particular movement vocabulary (e.g., plié, relevé, dégagé), which is an important part of the ballet-based workout (performing ballet-specific movements will build the ballet body).
- A proper warm-up and cool-down is an important part of any workout routine.
- Ballet-based workouts should be performed along with cardiovascular activities for best results and optimal fitness.
- Conventional fitness exercises combined with ballet exercises will lead to desirable changes in body shape and size.
- Both ballet and fitness exercises should be performed for a specific number of repetitions and on both sides of the body.

II

Lived Experiences of Ballet in
Contemporary Culture

4

MULTIPLE BODIES

In the Studio with Adolescent Ballet Dancers

Marianne I. Clark

Adolescent girls frequently cite dance as one of their favourite extracurricular and physical activities (Clark, Spence, & Holt, 2011; Dowda et al., 2009; Grieser et al., 2006). In studies of girls' physical activity experiences and preferences, girls describe dance as fun and as an outlet for self-expression. However, dance, particularly ballet, is also associated with an exceedingly thin body shape that has elicited critique from feminist dance scholars (Aalten, 2007; Foster, 1996; Green, 1999, 2001; Ritenburg, 2010; Thomas, 2003). Furthermore, health psychology researchers have reported correlations between the incidence of disordered eating and girls and women who study ballet, and point to pressure to achieve this elusive body as a contributing factor (Benn & Walters, 2001; Bettle, Bettle, Neumarker, & Neumarker, 2001; Nordin-Bates, Walker, & Redding, 2011; Penniment & Egan, 2012; Ravaldi et al., 2006). Feminist and health researchers are not the only ones provoked by the exceedingly slim idealized ballet body. As a former ballet dancer and current contemporary dancer, I have engaged in many conversations with fellow dancers, parents of young dancers, and non-dancers alike that reveal both a fascination and frustration with the narrowly defined ballet body ideal. In these conversations, the ballet body is lamented as being oppressive for young dancers and as a problematic celebration of a particular and circumscribed idea of desirable femininity. However, as dance continues to become more visible in contemporary society through the increasing popularity of dance-based television shows, movies, and even fitness workouts, the dancing body also becomes more visible and presents a fascinating topic of study.

To date, the dialogue in scholarly circles has largely revolved around the physical appearance of the ballet body. There is a persistent preoccupation with what this body looks like and less curiosity about what it does, how it moves, or about its experiences. Furthermore, the ballet body in question is the professional ballet body groomed for performance on professional stages. This ballet body faces different contextual realities and aesthetic demands than the bodies of dancers who dance in commercial (recreational) spaces and settings. In fact, little is known about the experiences of girls who dance in commercial settings. However, the proportion of girls who take dance lessons and become professional dancers is extremely small. For example, in 2011, national data showed only 8,100 Canadians reported dance (in a performance or teaching capacity) as their primary occupation (Hill Strategies, 2014). Yet it is estimated that over 625,000 Canadian girls participate in dance classes (Solutions Research Group, 2014). Therefore, as a dancer and feminist scholar, I wondered if there were ways to understand the ballet body beyond what it looks like and that exceed the salient image of the professional ballerina. I was curious about how non-elite ballet dancers understand their dancing bodies and how they might negotiate this strict ballet body aesthetic, if they do at all.

To address this curiosity, I conducted a research study that asked how adolescent girls who dance ballet in commercial (or recreational) dance studios understand their ballet bodies. In this chapter, I review the current literature on the professional ballet body and share results from a Foucauldian case study of one ballet class in a recreational dance studio in western Canada that identified multiple understandings of the ballet body beyond mere aesthetics.

The Elusive Ballet Bodily Ideal

Physical characteristics such as thinness, long limbs, and bodily delicacy characterize dominant understandings of the ballet body (Aalten, 2007; Foster, 1996; Green, 1999, 2001; Pickard, 2013; Ritenburg, 2010; Thomas, 2003). Indeed, the iconic image of the prima ballerina is easily conjured in the popular imagination and complies with this definition: the impossibly petite frame, the pink satin pointe shoes, and the almost always long hair pulled back into a neat bun cohere into a widely recognizable feminine archetype. Not only does her body comply with balletic ideals, but it is also the physical manifestation of conventional femininity (Foster, 1996).

Feminist dance scholars have historically focused their attention on this representational female ballet body and offered critiques of ballet as an oppressive practice for women (Aalten, 2007; Adair, 1992; Daly, 1987a, 1987b; Foster, 1996; Garafola, 1985; Novack, 1993). This critique has primarily identified ballet as a practice that "upholds the dominant ideology, for example, by continuing to select dancers on the basis of a classical ideal of beauty, by reinforcing traditional sex roles and by the hierarchical structures of both the training institutions and the ballet companies" (Adair, 1992, 88–89). Daly (1987a) further criticizes ballet because it is "rooted in an ideology which denies women their own agency" (17).

At the centre of these critiques is the prima ballerina's body, described as a "spectacle...the bearer and object of male desire" (Daly, 1987b, 57). Elaborate descriptions of this corporeal "spectacle" are woven into much of the feminist dance scholarship from the 1980s and 1990s. Through these writings we learn that the ballet body is "ephemeral" and conveys a "sumptuous ethereality" (Foster, 1996, 6), while being treated as a "submissive instrument" by male partners and the audience (Daly, 1987a, 14). Garafola (1985) provides this summary of the persistent ideology of the classical ballerina over time:

> The nineteenth century belongs to the ballerina. She haunts its lithographs and paintings, an ethereal creature touched with the charm of another age. Yet even when she turned into the fast, leggy ballerina of modern times, her ideology survived...The art of ballet...has yet to rid its aesthetic of yesterday's cult of the eternal feminine. Like her nineteenth-century forbearer, today's ballerina, an icon of teen youth, athleticism, and anorexic vulnerability, incarnates a feminine ideal defined overwhelmingly by men. (35)

This description captures several themes that run through the scholarship of this time and still persist, including the fascination with and objection to the objectification of the body, the link between ballet and eating disorders, and the reference to the oppressive ideology of masculine and feminine difference read primarily through the body. Indeed, ballet was thought to celebrate and reproduce the desirability of female delicacy, beauty, and fragility (Garafola, 1985). In addition, it was understood in opposition to masculine strength, athletic prowess, and virility (Adair, 1992; Daly, 1987b).

Ballet scholarship in the late 1990s extended this analysis and complicated the narrative of ballet as wholly oppressive and victimizing for female ballerinas (Aalten, 2004, 2007; Banes, 1998; Foster, 1996). These scholars sought to expand the analysis of the ideal ballet body by emphasizing the need to focus on the physical experiences of ballet dancers and their material, dancing bodies. In particular, Foster (1996) urged dance scholars to adopt a "more meat and bones approach to the body" (235), and Aalten (2004) suggested that the "instructional practices and the daily routines that create a dancer's body" require more attention (264).

Even more recently, scholars have turned their attention to the power mechanisms that shape the experiences of ballet and contemporary dancers (Green, 1999, 2001; Dryburgh & Fortin, 2010;

Fortin, Viera, & Tremblay, 2009; Ritenburg, 2010). For example, Fortin and colleagues (2009) examine how pre-professional contemporary dancers negotiate various dance discourses in relation to body and health issues. The authors defined discourse as "systems of thoughts composed of ideas, attitudes, beliefs, courses of action and practices that enable, just as they constrain, what can be said or done at particular times and places. Discourses construct current truth and what power relations they carry with them" (50). They continue to describe a dominant dance discourse, which values "an ideal body where aesthetic criteria of beauty, slimness, virtuosity, devotion and asceticism prevail" (Fortin et al., 2009, 50).

Similarly, in her studies with university ballet and contemporary dancers, Green (1999, 2001) critiques what she calls "dominant discourses" of dance that objectify the body and privilege a thin body above all else. Green does not define what these dominant discourses might be, but refers repeatedly to the idealized ballet body shape and size. In another Foucauldian study, Ritenburg (2010) examines the representations of the ballet body in popular culture and argues that the image of the extraordinary ballet body is reproduced in the popular and fitness media, children's books, and ballet academies and companies, sustaining connections between dominant understandings of ballet and idealized femininity. Ritenburg (2010) outlines how this type of body became normalized in the professional world of ballet and how it continues to be idealized in dance studios and popular culture through widespread discourses and practices.

When these scholars (Dryburgh & Fortin, 2010; Green, 1999, 2003; Ritenburg, 2010) draw upon Foucault's concept of discourse, they refer to "the ballet body" discourse to describe the specific bodily aesthetics (e.g., extreme thinness, long limbs) often idealized and celebrated in ballet. While this might be one interpretation of the term *discourse*, based on a closer reading of Foucault's work, I would argue that the ballet body itself is not a discourse, but, instead, that the ballet body is understood *through* a set of multiple discourses. It is these multiple ways of knowing about the ballet body in which I am interested. Therefore, in this chapter I expand upon the work of previous dance scholarship to identify the various meanings of the ballet body constructed by adolescent girls who dance in commercial settings.

A Foucauldian Understanding of Discourse

To begin my examination, I take up Foucault's (1972) definition of discourse. Foucault recognizes discourse as a system of beliefs and understandings that both enable and limit the way we come to know and talk about objects and social phenomena (Foucault, 1972; Markula & Pringle, 2006). Markula and Pringle (2006) explain that a Foucauldian understanding of discourse "refers to unwritten 'rules' that guide social practices and help to produce and regulate the production of statements that, correspondingly, control what can be understood and perceived but at the same time act to obscure" (31). In other words, discourse creates meaning systems through which we define our social world and ourselves. In my study, I am interested in the statements the dancers produce to talk about their understandings of the ballet body. Foucault (1978) is also interested in the link between discourse and the production of truth. He argues that some discourses become dominant and gain a status of "truth," while others are marginalized. In this way, discourse both enables and limits our understandings. In the case of this study, I examine what statements dominate the ways the dancers talk about the ballet body and, consequently, how they know the ballet body. Therefore, it is necessary to identify the multiple meanings that circulate in the ballet studio and to examine the "truths" they produce in order to glean insight into how girls understand their ballet bodies.

Foucault's (1978) concept of discourse is helpful for this study as he maintains that discourses are not fixed and are not understood as liberating or oppressive per se, but instead are linked closely to power relations. Foucault understands power as relational and fluid and as flowing through all relationships in contemporary society. Therefore, in a Foucauldian model, one individual or group does not "have" power that is used to oppress another individual or group; rather, all individuals have varying abilities to exercise power in relationships. Thus, in the case of young ballet dancers, Foucault would maintain that they are not oppressed by dance teachers or choreographers or by a particular understanding of the ballet body, but are part of a complex web of power relations and discursive practices. This study does not seek to identify one meaning of the ballet body as good or bad, liberating or oppressive. Nor does this study seek to uncover a "truth" about how girls understand their ballet bodies. Instead, I wish to examine the multiple ways in which young dancers understand their dancing bodies. As Foucault (1978) writes, "We must not imagine a world of discourses divided between accepted discourses and excluded discourses, or between the dominant discourse and the dominated one; but as a multiplicity of discursive elements that can come into play in various strategies" (100). Consequently, in this Foucauldian study, I examine how different meanings circulate within the specific power relations of the ballet studio, how they are taken up, and what practices they produce and reproduce. The research question guiding this study is, what meanings shape non-elite adolescent ballet dancers' understandings of their ballet bodies?

Methodology

To identify the statements of the ballet body drawn upon by female adolescent ballet dancers, I conducted semi-structured interviews with eleven ballet dancers in one advanced ballet class in a dance studio in western Canada. This study was part of a larger case study that was part of my doctoral research, which sought to understand how non-professional female ballet dancers construct a self through the dancing body. While the overarching case study utilized participant observation and semi-structured interviews to collect data and was guided by Foucault's theoretical axis of power, knowledge/discourse, and the self, this chapter reports on data collected from semi-structured interviews designed to further understand the girls' experiences with ballet.

Data were collected through multiple semi-structured interviews (Ellis, 1998; Hesse-Biber & Leavy 2011; Stake, 1995). As the researcher, I took an active role in the conversation (including sharing my own experiences) and sought to manage the direction of the interview to ensure conversations addressed the topics relevant to the research. The interviews ranged in duration from twenty-two to seventy-two minutes. Each interview was transcribed verbatim and analyzed using Foucault's theory as a guide. Pseudonyms were assigned to each participant to protect anonymity. This process helped me to develop a theoretically and empirically informed understanding of the multiple discourses that shape girls' understandings of the ballet body.

Recruitment and Sampling

The bounded case of study (Stake, 1995) was one advanced ballet class in one commercial dance studio in a large western Canadian city. This studio was selected according to the following criteria: dance classes were taught by professionally trained dance teachers; ballet was among the dance genres taught; and the studio did not explicitly position itself as a pre-professional studio, meaning it did not groom dancers for professional careers. Before collecting my empirical material, I obtained ethics approval from the University of Alberta Research Ethics Review Board.

Participants were selected according to criterion sampling (Patton, 2002). This term refers to the study of all participants who meet specific, predetermined criterion of importance. Sampling criteria included the following: age (fourteen to eighteen years), gender (female), at least two years of ballet training, and enrollment in two or more dance classes per week. These criteria helped ensure that studying ballet was an important aspect of the participants' lives and would be likely to inform their understandings and attitudes about their dancing bodies. All twelve girls who attended the advanced ballet class regularly were invited to participate. Because one girl stopped attending class early in the study, the final sample consisted of eleven female dancers between the ages of fourteen and eighteen. All participants studied only at the dance studio selected as the research site, attended two or more ballet classes a week, and studied three or more different genres of dance. Participants spent an average of 7.5 hours in dance class each week and, on average, had six previous years of ballet experience.

Negotiating Multiple Understandings of the Ballet Body

Conversations with the participants revealed nuanced and thoughtful reflections about the meanings of the ballet body in relationship to their own bodies. Instead of defining their bodies singularly according to the aesthetics of the idealized ballet body, participants actively negotiated multiple understandings about their dancing bodies.

Perfection Is the *Pointe*

Participants described the specific aesthetics of the ideal ballet body clearly and without hesitation. The most common descriptors included "thin" or "skinny" and "perfect." For example, Ella stated, "The ballerina body is crazy, super thin, with long legs and the perfect pointe." Rachel elaborated and described ballet bodies as "bodies that are just perfect in every way...skinny and delicate...If you go to the ballet none of the dancers have any hips and they are all really tiny and perfect looking."

These quotes revealed the importance of extreme slenderness to young dancers when defining the ballet body. In addition to being very thin, the ballet body was also referred to repeatedly as "perfect." In this context, the perfect ballet body was one that complied with an extensive checklist of specific aesthetic criteria for myriad body parts including hips, legs, arms, and feet. Cassie explained,

"Famous ballerinas are perfect in every way right down to their feet. They have long lean legs, delicate arms. They even have long graceful necks." Feet were commonly identified as an important part of the ballet body. Participants emphasized the importance of having high arches in the foot in order to achieve the ballet body ideal. Jess reflected, "Ballerinas have to have high arches...the feet are so important. You can have a beautiful body but without nice feet you'll never make it [professionally]." When asked why, she explained, "So much of ballet is about pointe work, and how the feet look on pointe...I don't know why but feet without high arches just don't look as good."

Dancers further explained how feet with high arches were important for creating the "nice lines" the ballet body is required to display. Cassie said, "You need to have nice long legs, but also good arches. It just makes the whole line look better." Rachel added, "When we dance...everything has to come together to create nice lines." When asked to explain what she meant by "nice lines," Rachel thought for a moment and elaborated: "Well, clean lines of the body...Ballet is all very precise and good technique creates good lines...Nice lines are what makes [sic] it so pretty...To have the best lines you need good extension and long legs and perfect feet."

Dryburgh and Fortin (2010) also suggest that the ability of professional dancers to create "beautiful lines" is a defining feature of the ballet body (98). Other dance scholars have similarly pointed to the importance of clean technique and nice lines (e.g., Pickard, 2013). However, "nice lines" as described by participants in this study were conveyed through the movement of the ballet body, not through the still body. In this way, the physical practice of ballet both builds and requires a certain type of body, one that performs movement with grace and exhibits aesthetically pleasing lines in movement. Consequently, the ballet body is more than a still body that complies with certain aesthetic criteria. It is a body that is required and able to move with a particular movement quality.

Putting Perfection in Its Place

Participants did not explicitly challenge the definition of the ideal ballet body as thin, aesthetically perfect, and graceful. In fact, dancers often understood their own bodies as non-compliant with this ideal, and consequently described their bodies as other than a "real" ballet body. Rachel explained it this way: "When I first look in the mirror, I usually think, 'oh I'm too big to be a real ballerina.'" Cassie shared, "Some days all I see is [sic] all my flaws and compare my body to the perfect, skinny ballerina...Those are the bad days." In these examples, the discourse of the precise aesthetics of the ballet body acted upon, shaped, and limited the girls' understandings of their own bodies as other than "real: dancing bodies. These findings echo Green (1999), who suggests that university dancers categorize themselves as something other than a "real" dancer based on their bodily aesthetics. Green's (1999) dancers believed that the only way to be a good dancer and to obtain praise and attention from the teacher was to attain this bodily ideal. This understanding of the stylized aesthetics of the ballet body was normalized and accepted as a "truth" by my participants.

However, participants did discuss ways in which they negotiated the stylized aesthetics. Cassie explained, "I know that I could look more like a real ballerina if I was super skinny, but I'm not trying to be famous, so as long as I'm able to keep up in class I don't really see the need." Violet added, "Maybe some people in class are a bit heavier, but it doesn't really matter. They're still amazing dancers." These reflections slightly disrupted the dominance of the aesthetics of the ballet body. The specific context in which the girls danced and the fact that they were not striving to be prima ballerinas created a discursive space that allowed for a multiplicity of acceptable dancing bodies. While the thin, aesthetically perfect ballet body was maintained and normalized as a desirable body, dancers expressed a certain acceptance of their own bodies by acknowledging their personal contextual realities (e.g., they were not training to be professional dancers). They argued that a range of bodies had the capacity to dance well and that learning and performing ballet were not conditional on attaining the perfect body. For example, Cassie noted, "I know I don't look like a 'real' dancer... but then, you know, after a while I just accept that...I mean I'm not a professional...but I'm still a good dancer." While Cassie did not overtly critique the narrowly defined ballet body, she acknowledged it was unnecessary for her circumstance, desires, and goals. She also acknowledged that she was "still, a good dancer and that her ballet body could perform in skilful ways, regardless of body size.

The Skilful Body

Many of the dancers described their own dancing bodies as skilful bodies. They described the impressive range of movement and movement qualities the ballet body was capable of demonstrating, and took pleasure in being able to move in skilful ways. Violet explained, "It's so amazing what dancers can do...from how high they can jump to how much control they have...It's [the ballet body] just so fine-tuned." Therefore, the ballet body was discursively understood as a skilful body. According to participants, the skilful body was one that demonstrated a high level of body awareness, was strong, co-ordinated, and able to perform complex movement.

When asked how they described their own ballet bodies, many participants explained their bodies were very "aware" bodies (Cassie, Rachel, Violet, Ella). When asked to elaborate on body awareness, participants often paused and considered their response, as though searching for adequate words. "I guess it's just knowing your body and where it is in space and being more careful in how you move it," explained Rachel. Violet further articulated, "It's like having good co-ordination all the time...As dancers we are more aware of the limits of our bodies and more aware of them when they move, of where our weight is...We can make different body parts do different things at the same time." Body awareness, therefore, referred to the overall co-ordination of the body and a heightened ability to know how to move the body in a space. Contemporary dancers in Markula's (2013) study also expressed the importance of body awareness and described it as an important aspect of their dancer identity.

The understanding of the ballet body as a skilled body also encompassed the body's ability to learn and perform complicated movements. In order to cultivate the skilful ballet body, girls celebrated the concepts of hard work and commitment. According to participants, hard work was demonstrated by the amount of time spent in the studio, persistent effort in class, and the ability to push themselves. When asked why it was important for dancers to push themselves, Violet answered, "Well, if you don't then you just stay the same and you never get to the next level. I always want to push myself, even when I'm so dead tired I just want to keep on dancing...If I'm not exhausted I feel like something's wrong; I'm not working hard enough." Violet's quote illustrates the normalization of hard work and pushing oneself in the dance studio, as well as the importance of reaching the "next level."

The necessity of hard work manifested as a code of behaviour that was understood and valued in the studio. This included taking multiple classes a week and being at the studio for multiple hours a night. When asked how a dancer demonstrated commitment, Rachel replied, "It's just like how much time you put in you know, [sic] like do you want to be out at the mall and stuff or do you want to dance?" In this study, all participants spent a lot of time at the studio (many upwards of ten hours per week). This was normal for them and they were proud of it. They described a great sense of connection to the studio and to their "dance family" (Sophia). Pickard (2013) also suggests that hard work and self-discipline are highly valued by young dancers who are striving to be professional dancers. However, in Pickard's (2013) study, engaging in hard work was perceived primarily as a means to attain the corporeal per-fection demanded by ballet. For my participants, hard work was discussed more evidently in relation to building skill and to achiev-ing the "next level" of ability. In fact, working at new skills was one of the girls' favourite aspects of dance and they took great pleasure in mastering new and more sophisticated movements. Many described learning new skills as "fulfilling" (Chloe, Violet, Rachel, Anne). Violet explained, "I like working at something, because after you get it, it becomes one more step you can use in the rest of your dancing and you can work off of it, and you feel a sense of accomplishment because you remember all the difficulties you went through to get there." Anne added, "It's just the best feeling when you know you're getting better...If I'm dancing well in class it can be my biggest accomplishment in a day...I love how working through something hard feels. It's exhilarating both physically and mentally." These quotes reveal that the process of mastering complicated movements results in pleasurable kinesthetic experiences and feelings of physical success. Mastering new steps also enabled dancers to develop a more expansive sophisticated movement repertoire, which was a very satisfying aspect of dance. Anne explained, "I love being able to perform harder choreography every year. It means my body can do more than it used to, and harder choreography is often more fun."

Millar (2013, see also Chapter 5 in this volume) also suggests that skill development is an important aspect of dance training for recreational contemporary dancers, and that progressively improving one's skills is part of what makes dance enjoyable. Similarly, dancers in Kolb and Kalogeropoulou's study (2012) reported that the presence of physical challenge was one of the main motivations to dance. Findings from my study support this previous research as hard work and skill development were closely related and perceived as positive by dancers. Additionally, while participants made distinctions between the aesthetics of "real" ballerina bodies and their own bodies, the understanding of the ballet body as a skilled body extended to their own bodies. Participants were proud of their good body awareness and were able to recognize the skill with which their bodies moved. As Violet alluded to earlier, dancers were able to control several different body parts at once, and their bodies faced multiple, often contradictory demands as they performed.

For example, Ella explained to me that flexibility (a highly valued aspect of the ballet body) was only productive when it was matched with strength: movement that required flexibility could look sloppy if it was not controlled. The height, freedom, and control of one leg as it swings in the hip joint, during a grand battement for example, depend on the stability and strength of the other leg. Therefore, dancers continuously work to accommodate complex cues and translate them into polished, effortless-looking movement. As Ella said, "We put the instructions the teacher gives us into our bodies." Therefore, engaging in ballet practices provided participants with multiple ways through which they can know their bodies and contributed to an understanding of a *doing* body, a body with great movement potential and capacity. The unique space and culture of this particular (recreational) studio facilitated experiences of success that were based primarily on movement capacity, not on body shape or size. Unlike previous dance research, which suggests that hard work is taken up solely to achieve a certain *looking* body (Gray & Kunkel, 2001; Green, 1999), participants in my study talked about hard work as a means to build a highly skilled *moving* body. However, dancers did not question the extreme extension so revered in ballet performance, or many of the other movements, such as high leaps, celebrated in ballet.

The Careful Body

In discussions about the ballet body, participants repeatedly introduced the idea of the ballet body as a "careful" body (Rachel, Anne, Chloe, Lily, Sophia, Ella). They explained learning challenging new movements very carefully in order to avoid injury. Ella maintained, "It takes a lot of concentration...and even though you just want to go for it, you have to be careful...Injuries can happen like that." Dancers also said they were generally mindful and careful about the way they took care of their bodies, both inside and outside of the studio. This sometimes impacted other physical practices and activities in which they engaged. Sophia participated in track and field at school and shared this reflection: "Whenever I'm doing track I always hear Mrs. M's voice in my head telling me to be careful," she laughed, "and I'm always thinking about my ballet body... Sometimes I don't put myself out there 100 per cent on the track because I'm afraid of injury." Most participants had experienced a dance-related injury of some kind ranging from rolled and sprained ankles, to a badly torn hamstring, to minor nagging injuries such as tight hips. Three had also experienced significant injuries outside of dance that impacted their dance training. They described the long road to recovery as an arduous one. "It took me almost a year to get back to where I was after my ankle healed," said Rachel, "and when I wasn't dancing I felt almost depressed...I don't know if I could handle another major injury."

Injuries among ballet dancers are not uncommon. In classical ballet companies, annual injury rates range from 55 to 95 per cent (Bronner, Ojofeitimi, & Rose, 2003; Nilsson, Leanderson, Wykman, & Strender, 2001; Thomas & Tarr, 2009). A growing body of scholarship examines ballet dancers' experience with pain and injury (Aalten, 2007; Pickard, 2007; Turner & Wainwright, 2003; Wainwright & Turner, 2004; Wulff, 1998). Much of this scholarship suggests that physical pain is normalized in the ballet context and that it is often ignored as the dancer perseveres in the pursuit of the ballet body. In this study, the teacher's body, which had achieved a high level of ballet certification, bore the signs of multiple injuries and her experiences exemplified the notion that pain is often ignored in elite dance settings. She had undergone knee and hip replacements and, as a result, demonstrated limited mobility in the classroom. This meant she was unable to demonstrate the movements and often called upon one of the most technically proficient dancers in the class to act as her demonstration body. However, as a result of her injuries, the teacher often instructed the dancers to be careful and emphasized the importance of good technique in preventing injury.

The Expressive Body

Finally, the girls revealed that the dancing body was also an expressive body. Participants articulated over and over again that being a good dancer requires more than strong technique and impressive extension; dancers must also be expressive and have the capacity to move the audience. As Jess explained, "Technique and expression are at the same level, because one can't be more important than the other. You don't want to watch someone who just has one. They depend on each other."

Therefore, dancing was about more than executing precise movement. There was an imperative to connect with those around them and to convey something energetic and affective to those watching, whether it was a full audience or simply the teacher. Dancers described the importance of expressing themselves through their bodies and the pleasure they derived from doing so. "It's a good thing I have dance, because I'm not great with words," said Cassie. When I asked her to explain, she continued, "I don't know...I just don't feel like I connect with people the best through talking... I express better through dance." Anne also said, "I don't really express myself well with words...It's like, I can just express more truthfully through dance." When asked to elaborate, Anne thought for a moment and said, "Well, it's sort of that sometimes feelings or something that you feel doesn't have a word to go with it...Like if I try to explain to someone how I feel it's never really how I feel... So with dance it's just more true." Several dancers said that dance helped them describe moods and states of being that could not "be put into words." It was as though naming how they felt inherently limited or failed to capture what it was girls felt or experienced: there was never the right word or adequate words. Yet it is through words that our society primarily communicates and functions. Therefore, I suggest that participant reflections about the inability of language to capture what they experience and express through dance points to the reliance we have on language and text in contemporary society, and the resulting limitations.

Furthermore, participants struggled to describe their dance experiences through named, identifiable emotions. Emotions are often understood categorically and narrowly, and might not always capture the nuances or complexity of what the dancers might feel (Massumi, 1995). Ella shared, "It's so hard to put into words, because sometimes I'll hear music that is sort of sad and slow, and I'll feel a bit sad when I'm dancing, almost like an ache...but at the same time I'm joyful because I'm moving to such beautiful music." Through dance she is able to convey this "messy" expressive state without having to name a particular emotion. Dance also allowed participants to express a wide range of emotions that might not be appropriate or easy to express in other settings. Jess elaborated: "I love dance, because you get to be so many different things in it. One piece might be sad and slow, so you might express something that you're sad about, but then you can also be like crazy and almost angry, or funny." When asked if she could be like that in other areas of her life, Jess said, "Um, well, not really, because everyone kind of expects you to be one way...I couldn't really be like crazy or bad at school, my teachers would be shocked [laughs]...So I guess that's what I like about dance: I get to experiment."

This bodily expression also facilitated unique ways of connecting with others. Violet shared this anecdote: "My Mum came to our show, and she doesn't really like understand why I love dance so much...So, I just decided I would throw myself into it, just 120 per cent...and I danced so hard and put so much into it, I was actually crying on stage...and afterwards my Mum gave me a big hug and said 'Wow, I think I get it now.'" These quotes reveal that dancers created relationships and shared experiences with those around them in non-verbal ways and without articulating defined emotions. Through dance they were able to express aspects of their selves that shaped their relationships with other dancers and family members in inarticulable ways. This ability to express, although difficult to put into words, was important to the dancers.

Conclusion

While feminist dance scholarship has emphasized and critiqued the oppressive nature of the idealized ballet body (Aalten, 2007; Adair, 1992; Daly, 1987a, 1987b; Foster, 1996; Garafola, 1985; Green, 1999, 2001; Thomas, 2003), this study revealed multiple, less dominant meanings that flourished in the dance studio, and enabled a slightly more spacious understanding of the ballet body that exceeded aesthetics. Participants actively negotiated the meanings that informed their understanding of the ballet body and took pleasure in both the doing of ballet and in the knowledge and recognition of their physical skill. This is not to assert that the idealized, thin ballet body was not a noticeable presence in our conversations and in the studio. Indeed, it haunted this project. Yet the understandings and experiences of the dancing body were not adequately captured or conveyed through the corporeal perfection alone. Participants pointed to more capacious and productive understandings of their dancing bodies as aware, skilful, and expressive bodies, and to the "in-between" spaces their dancing bodies allowed them to inhabit, not otherwise accessible to them in other movement or social settings.

This project, therefore, points to further ways of knowing the ballet body that may hold potential to complicate the dominant understanding of the ballet bodily ideal as simply corporeal perfection. These multiple meanings may be mobilized to further disrupt the understanding of the ballet body as impossibly thin and perfect. This is not to say that multiple meanings do not exist alongside each other. However, allowing for multiple understandings might alleviate the dominance of one understanding. For example, although, the thin, idealized ballet body was discussed and sometimes coveted by participants in this study, these dancers generally did not perceive the need to attain this body to be particularly relevant to them. In conversations, it became evident that they had other stories to tell that they perceived as more interesting. For example, they were interested in and committed to building a skilled body. However, the skilled body was still defined along the lines of normalized ballet vocabulary and the ability to perform extreme movements. Yet the understanding of the ballet body as corporeal perfection existed alongside the low murmur of many other understandings. Participants spoke animatedly about the skilled body, thoughtfully about the careful body, and passionately about the expressive body. For participants, the idealized, dominantly represented ballet body was negotiated and put into relief by their own moving bodies: bodies that were physically skilled, that derived pleasure from physical accomplishment and mastery, and that had a profound capacity for expression and relating to others in nonverbal ways.

Additionally, given the dancers' and my own struggle to articulate and understand the expressive body more clearly and coherently, I propose that perhaps we do not have words or language that is spacious enough to accommodate this bodily force, this bodily capacity for expression and connection. The kinesthetic tension and seeming contradiction of the very physical, energetic practices required in dance (reflected in such cues given by the dance teacher as "push down through your supporting leg and send your other leg up") may in some way create spaces and ways of being that I call "in-between." This concept of being in-between manifests in physical practices, bodily movement, and even the girls' subjectivities (selves). When dancing, the girls could exist in-between emotions. Perhaps in this particular socio-political and historic moment, the repertoire or vocabulary related to body, movement, and expression available to girls is limited and limiting. Perhaps in the studio they have access to a more satisfactory or productive repertoire of practices.

In conclusion, I argue that we must not celebrate nor critique ballet or the ballet body unreflectively or universally, but instead submit it to a deeply contextual analysis. It is important to note that this small study captured the experiences of white, middle-class girls for whom attending regular ballet class was

economically and practically feasible. It also captured one recreational studio and so reflected the ways of understanding the
ballet body and power relations in which this particular studio is
embedded. However, it does offer multiple understandings of the
ballet body that afford a reprieve from the dominant aesthetic
ideal. Perhaps ballet teachers, choreographers, and others who
teach physical movement in organized settings may reflect on the
multiple meanings that emerged in this study and consider how
one might offer and create movement spaces and practices that
allow for multiple understandings of moving bodies. These understandings may expand young girls' field of possibilities for positive
movement experiences and accommodate a forceful, energetic,
doing body.

References

Aalten, A. (2004). "The moment when it all comes together": Embodied
experiences in ballet. *European Journal of Women's Studies, 11*(3), 263–76.
doi:10.1177/1350506804044462

Aalten, A. (2007). Listening to the dancer's body. *The Sociological Review, 55*
(Supp. 1), 109–25.

Adair, C. (1992). *Women and dance: Sylphs and sirens.* London: MacMillan.

Banes, S. (1998). *Dancing women: Female bodies on stage.* London: Routledge.

Benn, T., & Walters, D. (2001). Between Scylla and Charybdis. Nutritional education
versus body culture and the ballet aesthetic: The effects on the lives of female
dancers. *Research in Dance Education, 2*, 139–54.

Bettle, N., Bettle, O., Neumarker, U., & Neumarker, K. J. (2001). Body image and self-
esteem in adolescent ballet dancers. *Perceptual and Motor Skills, 93*, 297–309.

Bronner, S., Ojofeitimi, S., & Rose, D. (2003). Injuries in a modern dance company:
Effect of comprehensive management on injury incidence and time loss. *The
American Journal of Sports Medicine, 31*, 365–73.

Clark, M., Spence, J. C., & Holt, N. L. (2011). In the shoes of young adolescent girls:
Understanding physical activity experiences through interpretive description.
Qualitative Research in Sport and Exercise, 3, 193–210.

Daly, A. (1987a). The Balanchine woman: Of hummingbirds and channel swimmers.
The Drama Review, 31, 8–21.

Daly, A. (1987b). Classical ballet: A discourse of difference. *Women & Performance: A
Journal of Feminist Theory, 3*, 57–66.

Dowda, M., Dishman, R. K., Porter, D., Saunders, R. P., & Pate, R. R. (2009).
Commercial facilities, social cognitive variables, and physical activity of

12th grade girls. *Annals of Behavioral Medicine: A Publication of the Society of Behavioral Medicine, 37*, 77–87.

Dryburgh, A., & Fortin, S. (2010). Weighing in on surveillance: Perception of the impact of surveillance on female ballet dancers' health. *Research in Dance Education, 11*, 95–108.

Ellis, J. (1998). Narrative inquiries with children and youth. In J. Ellis (Ed.), *Teaching from understanding: Teacher as interpretive inquirer* (33–56). New York: Garland.

Fortin, S., Viera, A., & Tremblay, M. (2009). The experience of discourses in dance and somatics. *Journal of Dance and Somatic Practices, 1*, 47–64.

Foster, S. L. (1996). *Choreography and narrative: Ballet's staging of story and desire.* Bloomington: Indiana University Press.

Foucault, M. (1972). *The archaeology of knowledge and the discourse on language.* (A. M.Sheridan Smith, Trans.). New York: Pantheon Books.

Foucault, M. (1978). *The history of sexuality. (Volume 1: An Introduction).* (R. Hurley, Trans.). New York: Pantheon Books.

Garafola, L. (1985). The travesty dancer in nineteenth-century ballet. *Dance Research Journal, 12*, 35–40.

Gray, K. M., & Kunkel, M. A. (2001). The experience of female ballet dancers: A grounded theory. *High Ability Studies, 12*(1), 7–25.

Green, J. (1999). Somatic authority and the myth of the ideal body in dance education. *Dance Research Journal, 31*, 80–89.

Green, J. (2001). Socially constructed bodies in American dance classrooms. *Research in Dance Education, 2*, 155–73.

Green, J. (2003). Foucault and the training of docile bodies in dance education. *The Journal of the Arts and Learning Special Interest Group of the American Education Research Association, 19*, 99–125.

Grieser, M., Vu, M. B., Bedimo-Rung, A. L., Neumark-Sztainer, D., Moody, J., Young, D. R., & Moe, S. G. (2006). Physical activity attitudes, preferences, and practices in African American, Hispanic, and Caucasian girls. *Health Education and Behavior, 33*, 40–51.

Hesse-Biber, S. N., & Leavy, P. (2011). *The practice of qualitative research.* Thousand Oaks, CA: Sage.

Hill Strategies Research Inc. (2014). A statistical profile of artists and cultural workers in Canada. Retrieved from http://www.hillstrategies.com/content/statistical-profile-artists-and-cultural-workers-canada

Kolb, A., & Kalogeropoulou, S. (2012). In defence of ballet: Women, agency and the philosophy of pleasure. *Dance Research, 30*, 107–25.

Markula, P. (2013). (Im)Mobile bodies: Contemporary semi-professional dancers' experiences with injury. *International Review for the Sociology of Sport, 50*(7), 840–64. doi:10.1177/1012690213495745

Markula, P., & Pringle, R. (2006). *Foucault, sport and exercise: Power, knowledge and transforming the self.* New York: Routledge.

Massumi, B. (1995). The autonomy of affect. *Cultural Critique, 31*, 83–109.

Millar, C. (2013). "Moving for pleasure": The positive experiences of women in contemporary dance (Unpublished master's thesis). University of Alberta, Edmonton.

Nilsson, C., Leanderson, J., Wykman, A., & Strender, L. E. (2001). The injury panorama in a Swedish professional ballet company. Knee Surgery, Sports Traumatology, Arthroscopy, 9, 242–46.

Nordin-Bates, S. M., Walker, I. J., & Redding, E. (2011). Correlates of disordered eating attitudes among male and female young talented dancers: Findings from the UK Centres for Advanced Training. Eating Disorders, 19, 211–33.

Novack, C. (1993). Ballet, gender and cultural power. In H. Thomas (Ed.), Dance, gender and power (34–48). London: MacMillan.

Patton, M. Q. (2002). Qualitative research and evaluation methods (3rd ed.). Thousand Oaks, CA: Sage.

Penniment, K. J., & Egan, S. J. (2012). Perfectionism and learning experiences in dance class as risk factors for eating disorders in dancers. European Eating Disorders Review, 20, 13–22.

Pickard, A. (2007). Girls, bodies and pain: Negotiating the body in ballet. In I. Wellard (Ed.), Re-thinking gender and youth sport (36–50). London: Routledge.

Pickard, A. (2013). Ballet body belief: Perceptions of an ideal ballet body from young ballet dancers. Research in Dance Education, 14, 3–19.

Ravaldi, C., Vannacci, A., Bolognesi, E., Mancini, S., Faravelli, C., & Ricca, V. (2006). Gender role, eating disorder symptoms, and body image concern in ballet dancers. Journal of Psychosomatic Research, 61, 529–35.

Ritenburg, H. M. (2010). Frozen landscapes: A Foucauldian genealogy of the ideal ballet dancer's body. Research in Dance Education, 11(1), 71–85.

Solutions Research Group. (2014, June 10). Massive competition in pursuit of the $5.7 billion Canadian youth sports market. Retrieved from http://www.srgnet.com/2014/06/10/massive-competition-in-pursuit-of-the-5-7-billion-canadian-youth-sports-market/

Stake, R. E. (1995). The art of case study research. Thousand Oaks, CA: Sage.

Thomas, H. (2003). The body, dance and cultural theory. New York: Palgrave Macmillan.

Thomas, H. & Tarr, J. (2009). Dancer's perceptions of pain and injury: Positive and negative effects. Journal of Dance Medicine & Science, 13(2), 51–59.

Turner, B. S., & Wainwright, S. P. (2003). Corps de ballet: The case of the injured ballet dancer. Sociology of Health & Illness, 25, 269–88.

Wainwright, S. P., & Turner, B. S. (2004). Epiphanies of embodiment: Injury, identity and the balletic body. Qualitative Research, 4, 311–37.

Wulff, H. (1998). Ballet across borders: Career and culture in the world of dancers. New York: Berg.

5

"MOVING FOR PLEASURE"

The Positive Experiences of Ballet Dancers Moving into Recreational
Contemporary Dance

Carolyn Millar

I entered the field of dance research to explore the experiences of women in recreational dance training. Trained in a ballet school and a private studio, I am currently dancing with a contemporary university dance group. While I have had positive and valuable experiences from both ballet and contemporary dance, I became particularly interested in how other dancers with previous ballet training discover and adjust to a recreational dance environment with a strong focus on contemporary dance. This recreational dance community is now a large part of my social circle and continues to be the source of many important friendships and role models in my life. While I continue to see much joy, passion, and dedication to dance in my community, when I read the research on women's experiences in dance it tends to focus on the negative outcomes of dance participation, particularly in ballet.

If the effects and emotions associated with ballet training are largely perceived as negative and harmful, as the research suggests, what keeps women returning to dance even after their ballet training in studio settings has ended? The purpose of my research is to uncover some of the positive experiences of continued dance training when transferring to a different dance form in a different environment. By exploring the individual dance experiences of trained ballet dancers who are now dancing contemporary dance in a recreational setting, we can gain insight into the experiences that inspire continued involvement in a different form of dance. With significant previous training, participants in my study had a wealth of ballet-related experiences against which to reflect upon their current training. Before highlighting these experiences, I first review the previous literature on negative and positive experiences in ballet training. I then outline my interview methods and my phenomenological approach, and continue with a discussion of my findings regarding the positive experiences of ballet-trained dancers' continued participation in contemporary dance. In summary, I illustrate how their responses can help us understand what conditions may be ideal for highly trained ballet dancers who are seeking to continue with recreational contemporary dance in adulthood.

Ballet: Negative or Positive Experience for Women?

As I indicated, there is substantial literature on negative experiences of ballet participation. Negative experiences include those interpreted to be physically, psychologically, or emotionally detrimental. These experiences can include disordered eating behaviours and attitudes, maladaptive perfectionism, anxiety, injury, and the perpetuation of female stereotypes (Aalten, 2005; de Bruin, Bakker, & Oudejans, 2009; Gray & Kunkel, 2001; Nordin-Bates, Walker, & Redding, 2011; Penniment & Egan, 2010; Thomas & Tarr, 2009; Walker & Nordin-Bates, 2010).

Negative Experiences in Ballet Training
Dance studies researchers have examined eating disorders, restrictive eating behaviours, and body dissatisfaction as negative

experiences. In studies of dancers' psychology, dancers' personalities have been found to interact with their training environments to create perceptions that can increase the risk for eating disorders (de Bruin et al., 2009, Nordin-Bates et al., 2011; Penniment & Egan, 2010). Participants reported internalizing norms associated with the ideal ballet body, including expectations of restrictive eating and rewards for slenderness (Benn & Walters, 2001; Penniment & Egan, 2010). The ballet dancers, then, perceived instruction on obtaining and maintaining slender figures as an essential part of their dance education. Further, Nordin-Bates et al. (2011) investigated perfectionism in contemporary and ballet dancers, and found that dancers who exhibited negative traits associated with perfectionism were more likely to experience low self-esteem and eating disorders. Ballet dancers have also been found to have high body dissatisfaction, which impacts their self-image and ultimately makes dance class less enjoyable (Alexias & Dimitropoulou, 2011; Benn & Walters, 2001; Dryburgh & Fortin, 2010).

In addition to body image problems and disordered eating, ballet dancers' emotions, perceptions, and thoughts are critical to understanding dance experiences. In their interviews, Bond and Stinson (2007) found that fear, embarrassment, feelings of inferiority, and disengagement emerged strongly in young ballet students' responses to their dance training. In their study of professional ballet dancers and university-aged ballet students, Benn and Walters (2001) argue that dance instructors, directors, and choreographers have ultimate authority over a dancer and use their power to transmit ideas of the ideal physique, culture-specific phenomena (including traditional hierarchies), and gender. Several researchers interpreted the authoritarian nature of ballet training as harmful as it was detrimental to the dancers' autonomy and contributed to their objectification (Benn & Walters, 2001; Dryburgh & Fortin, 2010; Dyer, 2010; Gray & Kunkel, 2001; McEwen & Young, 2011; Pickard, 2012). With so many possible detrimental effects, what is known about the ballet dancers' personal experiences of enjoyment and desire to dance?

Positive Experiences in Ballet Training

Dancers return year after year, whether professionally or recreationally, to the dance classroom despite possible negative experiences. This speaks to the multidimensional nature of dance: it serves as a source of positive experiences that offset or overpower any negative effects. Positive experiences relate to emotional benefits, enjoyment, and both physical and mental pleasure. I found that ballet dancers' accounts of the enjoyable, pleasurable aspects of dance are underrepresented in the current dance research. Dance researchers Kolb and Kalogeropoulou (2012), who focus on recreational ballet training, believe this underrepresentation is problematic. "However," they write, "we believe that these perspectives are one-sided, ignoring as they do an evaluation of ballet as pleasurable sensory activity, and moreover reinforcing the apparent prejudice against pleasure in much Western thought" (Kolb & Kalogeropoulou, 2012, 111). In contrast to the findings of authoritarian ballet culture, Fisher (2007), Kolb and Kalogeropoulou (2012), and Pickard and Bailey (2009) focus on ballet dancers' personal agency and enjoyment. For example, Fisher (2007) recalls, "I had experienced ballet as a positive force in my life, a tool that had facilitated my learning about personal agency, collaborative effort, and spiritual expansion" (4). Fisher felt empowered by ballet where she experienced a sense of community and well-being. Pickard and Bailey (2009) suggest that such passion and commitment to dance may be fueled by the accumulation of positive experiences: "The young dancer is likely to experience success, challenge and disappointment but it is important that the dancer perceives the positive outweighing the negative" (178) to continue their participation. For example, the ballet dancers of Pickard and Bailey's (2009) research experienced pain and injury, rejection at auditions, and failure to obtain certain skills, but they did not frame these occurrences in a negative way. Instead, dancers focused on positive experiences of achievements and successes that followed, attributing their perseverance to their love of ballet and personal determination. Young ballet students in Bond and Stinson's (2007) study also reported high engagement, a sense of accomplishment, meaning, satisfaction, and emotional connection related to their dance classes.

Kolb and Kalogeropoulou (2012) found that women with long-time recreational engagement in ballet exhibited devotion to the activity and enjoyed its discipline. The adult recreational ballet dancers in Kolb and Kalogeropoulou's (2012) study were physically, emotionally, and mentally involved in ballet participation. They enjoyed the challenge of their classes, thrived on the discipline and structure of them, and took pleasure in the degree of difficulty in ballet training. The challenge motivated them, and thus they perceived overcoming the challenge as a reward in itself. Working with discipline and being challenged provided the framework for achievement and progression in dance, and led to further enjoyment and feelings of success (Kolb & Kalogeropoulou, 2012). There was, however, a crucial difference from professional dance environments: "Vitally, this distinguishes people for whom dance is a recreational pursuit from professional dancers; for the latter dance ceases to be a relief from work and instead constitutes the very essence of their labours" (Kolb & Kalogeropoulou, 2012, 114).

Contrary to reports of disordered eating in professional ballet culture, recreational and contemporary dancers often reported improved body image and self-esteem (Burgess, Grogan, & Burtwitz, 2006; Green, 2001; Lewis & Scannell, 1995). Compared to ballet or professional dance, the training environment of contemporary and recreational dance supports more collaboration, co-operation, intrinsic motivation, and self-expression (Alter, 1997; Andrzejewski, 2009; Huddy & Stevens, 2011; Mainwaring & Krasnow, 2010; Vertinsky, 2010). However, the "most difficult to hear are the voices of the young, the inexperienced, the less technically fluent, the locally and regionally based artists—in other words the vast majority of participants in dance activity" (Bracey, 2004, 7). I aim to hear some of these voices in my research.

In summary, while ballet participation in particular can generate negative experiences such as body image problems and low self-esteem, it can also be a source of enjoyment, accomplishment, emotional satisfaction, and social connection. In addition, research has often focused on pre-professional ballet training (e.g., Pickard & Bailey, 2009; McEwen & Young, 2011) or professional ballet (e.g., Turner & Wainwright, 2003; Wainwright & Turner, 2004), while there is less research on recreational ballet dancers' experiences (e.g., Kolb & Kalogeropoulou, 2012). Although contemporary dance and recreational ballet have been found to provide more positive influence than the professional ballet world, there is little research on studio-trained ballet dancers who transition to recreational contemporary dance to continue to dance. My focus is on positive experiences of trained ballet dancers, and I want to explore specifically contemporary dance in the recreational setting, where previous researchers have found a supportive environment. To identify such positive dance experiences, I chose a phenomenologically inspired, interpretive approach in my study.

Phenomenologically Inspired Interpretive Approach to Positive Dance Experiences

My purpose is to explore the positive experiences of ballet-trained dancers continuing their training through contemporary dance. I earlier conceptualized positive dance experiences as those that are enjoyable, physically exhilarating, benefit well-being, and/or elicit emotions such as happiness, joy, or contentment. However, such a definition only illustrates my own subjective experiences of transitioning from being a studio-trained ballet dancer to a recreational contemporary dancer. To understand what positive dance experiences mean for other women, I left the interpretation and description of a "positive experience" up to the participants. I was further interested in how positive experiences fuel their commitment to continue dance, albeit in a different setting, and the benefits they perceive from their involvement.

I chose to approach my research from the interpretive perspective (Markula & Silk, 2011). Within the interpretive paradigm, research is understood as a subjective and interactive process, and all knowledge production is acknowledged to be subjective. Thus, my approach to exploring positive dance experiences served to "expose and discuss the experiences of individuals rather than ascertain 'truth'" (Bracey, 2004, 8). Embracing relativist ontology, the interpretive researcher believes that multiple meanings of reality are constructed by different individuals, and thus the representation of reality through research is a co-construction between researcher and participants (Markula & Silk, 2011). Consequently, in my study, I considered myself, as a dancer/researcher, to be exploring positive dance experiences together with my participants.

To better understand participants' experiences and interpret their meanings, I drew from phenomenology. Phenomenology has been used by several dance studies scholars to capture the multiple meanings of dancers' experiences (Alexias & Dimitropoulou, 2011; Bond & Stinson, 2007; Bracey, 2004; Fraleigh, 2000; Jackson, 2005; Parviainen, 2002; Rouhiainen, 2008). Fraleigh (2000) believes phenomenology, instead of distancing the researcher from participants, allows for representation of the voice of the dancer, choreographer, and teacher together with the dance researcher's voice. In this sense, phenomenology is compatible with my interpretive research approach. Parviainen (2002) adds that the work of phenomenologists is particularly insightful because its focus on physical perception can illuminate dance as a physical pursuit. From a phenomenological perspective, the dancer's knowledge and experience are in part shaped by their perceptions of their body, which in turn influence their movements (Parviainen, 2002). According to Bond and Stinson (2007), phenomenological descriptions form a collection of sources that can be examined systematically to provide a robust picture of experiences of dancing within a certain group. However, it is not possible, through phenomenological study, to conclusively compare dancers from different populations. In my research, I provide a picture of the lived experiences of a very specific group of dancers: highly trained, studio-trained ballet dancers who continue their dance training within a university-based recreational contemporary dance company.

A phenomenologically inspired, interpretive approach influenced by Merleau-Ponty encompasses what I deem to be the most valuable elements of this research: the experiences of contemporary female dancers, my personal dance experience, and what these experiences may contribute to the understanding of dance. Fraleigh (2000), Parviainen (2002), and Bracey (2004) (who follows the interpretations of Fraleigh [2000]) count Merleau-Ponty, an existential phenomenology theorist, among their major influences. According to Allen-Collinson (2009), Merleau-Ponty is also a commonly referenced theorist in phenomenological approaches to physical culture. Merleau-Ponty's phenomenological approach is especially suited for researching physical cultures such as sport and dance because of the focus on embodiment. Dance is a physical pursuit that places much significance on body awareness, aesthetics, and the mind–body connection. The onus on the body and its connection to the consciousness makes existential phenomenology particularly effective for uncovering the meanings in the human experience of dance (Allen-Collinson, 2009). This approach also accounts for the influence of a researcher's subjective involvement. Thus, my own subjectivity as a researcher and as a dancer with long-standing relationships with the ballet studio community is accepted as a necessary part of the research. Bond and Stinson (2007) further described this approach to dance research: "We do not have, and can never have, 'the whole picture' of what dance means to any one child or group of young people. Because it is constantly in the process of creation, meaning is always partial...We acknowledge ourselves as both creators and discoverers of meaning" (157). By acknowledging my own subjectivity as a researcher, a creator and discoverer of meaning, I was also self-reflexive and acknowledged the influence of my personal experiences on the research. Personally, I have a wealth of positive experiences related to my participation in both ballet and contemporary dance training. These experiences are valuable to my identity as a dancer, instructor, and professional working within community recreation. I acknowledge, however, that not all individuals have positive experiences in dance training. Similarly, the unique nature of experience means that not all positive experiences are the same, and meanings of a positive experience may differ between the researcher and participants.

Methods

My main research questions were, what dance training experiences are interpreted as positive experiences by highly trained studio ballet dancers who continue to dance as contemporary dancers in a recreational setting? And how do dancers overcome challenges when transitioning from the ballet studio setting to recreational, contemporary dance training? I conducted semi-structured interviews with open-ended questions (Markula & Silk, 2011) to answer these research questions. The hour-long interviews took place at a set time at the participants' convenience and at the office of the on-campus dance studio. I developed the interview guide based on my reading of the previous literature to ask dancers to reflect on their previous ballet experiences and their current dance participation. Interviews were recorded via audio device and transcribed for analysis.

My analysis was based on meaning condensation, a process developed by Kvale and Brinkmann (2007) and derived from the phenomenological analysis of Giorgi (1975). Following a philosophical understanding of phenomenology by focusing on the meanings of the interviews (Kvale & Brinkmann, 2009), in this analysis "long statements are compressed into brief statements in which the main sense of what is said is rephrased in a few words" (Kvale & Brinkmann, 2007, 205). My analysis consisted of five main steps: reading the interview through, determining "natural meaning units," identifying dominant themes, linking meaning units to purpose of study, and establishing a descriptive statement based on the essential themes (Kvale & Brinkmann, 2007). This study obtained approval by the Research Ethics Board of the University of Alberta.

Participants

Like qualitative research in general, I used purposive sampling, more specifically convenience sampling (Markula & Silk, 2011) to collect my interview data. Further criterion sampling (Markula & Silk, 2011) of dancers ensured the women met criteria of having previous and substantial ballet experience in pre-professional, vocational, or private studio settings prior to their involvement with the university dance group and were eighteen years of age or older. Participant recruitment was carried out through in-class announcements and an email listserv.

Eight female participants volunteered and were interviewed (see the Appendix at the end of the chapter). The dancers' involvement in the university-based dance group ranged from approximately 1 year to 6 years at the time of interviews. The average age of participants was 25.25 years, ranging from 18 to 36 years. The average years of dance participation was 19 years. The dancers were all current participants in contemporary dance and, besides ballet, had previous experience in jazz, tap, hip hop, and/or musical theatre. In the following discussion, I refer to the participants by pseudonyms to ensure their anonymity.

Results and Discussion

My analysis is based on the ballet dancers' own understanding of how contemporary dance continues to be a positive factor in their lives. The majority of their experiences were complementary to the definition of positive dance experience established by existing literature: it was emotionally significant, enjoyable, pleasurable, and psychologically or physically beneficial. Each of the three main themes also has three subthemes that illustrate the complexity of positive dance experience:

1. Positive physical experience
   • physicality

- emotional connection to movement
- skill mastery

2. Positive experiences related to dance identity
   - dance identity
   - changes to dance identity
   - commitment to dance

3. Recreational dance environment
   - recreational dance
   - interpersonal aspects of recreational dance
   - influence of the instructor

Positive Physical Experiences

One of the most prominent themes was the importance of the physical experience of dancing when transitioning from ballet training in a studio to contemporary dance. By exploring the centrality of movement, I follow other dance phenomenologists to acknowledge dancing as a way of knowing and the centrality of movement, and the body, on dancers' experiences (Fraleigh, 2000; Parviainen, 2002).

The dancers' perceptions of their bodies and movement were valuable to understanding their decision to continue dancing in a different dance style and setting. Contemporary dance provided opportunities to enjoy moving and being physical. Some interviewees described feelings of freedom and power when they, once again, were able to "take up space" through their movement, move in "big ways," and explore their physicality in their contemporary dance classes. Sara said her favourite part of class was to "feel my body move through space and take up as much room as I can. There's something really powerful about that." Danielle referred to "conquering" the space with her movement while others expressed feeling free when they move. Unlike professional or pre-professional ballet dancers (Dryburgh & Fortin, 2010; Gray & Kunkel, 2001), these recreational dancers did not appear to be turning into docile bodies dancing in an authoritarian setting. In addition, many of the dancers believed that in contemporary dance, how their bodies moved was more important than how their bodies looked. Amanda, who had previously trained strictly in ballet, explained that her body experience through contemporary dance was "really positive because...it was really empowering for me to see that I can have any body shape and still dance with it." Sara added, "I love my body!... You have to respect your body and the way it moves, what it can do...I don't think it's so much how my body physically looks but what it does for me and it works pretty well." Learning new ways to move increased awareness of how the dancers' bodies felt and moved. Danielle explained that her current involvement in contemporary dance helped in "realizing the benefits of dance in terms of how your body works, understanding your body, and I think that feels good to me. That's just an amazing feeling when you understand every move in a better way."

Perceived fitness and health gains were also important aspects of the physical experience of continued dance practice for my interviewees. For example, such health-related aspects as "stretching" (Karen), "the feeling of being stronger" (Chloe), "strength" (Sara), "a good workout" (Emily), and "getting sweaty" (Jamie) were important for these dancers. For Emily, the benefits of dance as physical activity were influential throughout her life: "I feel good being able to be active...You feel better physically, a bit more in shape, but it also makes you happy, makes you social so generally a positive influence on your self-esteem." Being physically active influenced the dancers' health habits, and some cited learning about nutrition, eating, and healthy choices through their current involvement in dance. Chloe remarked, "I feel like dance has made me eat better because I want to do better and I want to be more fit and so I think it motivates [me] to make other healthy choices in my lifestyle outside of dance."

The interviewees could have chosen to take part in a different form of physical activity (e.g., sport or exercise) after continuing with their studio became unfeasible. However, emotional connection to movement marked a distinct and important difference between dance and other physical activities. Jamie explained, "Dance can be overlooked because sports and things are what most people know but I think expressive movement is important too." Danielle also spoke to the emotional expression of dance: "Emotionally, the body has so many ways to experience and express emotion and that's why I dance because it feels good...It makes us feel something. It's not just about the technical aspect of it." Danielle further explained the importance of expressive movement in dance: "I'm dancing. And it feels like you're moving for pleasure and not for training." The emotional connection to movement was most often described as "release." Release in their contemporary dance setting meant stress relief, an emotional outlet, and relaxation. In this study, the participants saw dance as an opportunity to "let go" (Amanda), "let loose" (Emily), and "decompress" (Jamie). When able to dance, their mood improved, they felt happier, more optimistic, and coped better with stressors.

The dancers participated in an advanced level of contemporary dance, and thus their training consisted of complex physical skills and high levels of fitness. According to Kolb and Kalogeropoulou (2012), adult women involved in recreational ballet took pleasure in the degree of difficulty. My findings were similar. For example, Sara recalled a particular instance of a challenging ballet barre exercise from her training: "I loved that feeling of just pushing yourself to get...through the whole exercise...which was really challenging...but in a way people could succeed...and you feel like you conquered this amazing goal." She continued to seek challenges: "Sometimes...I can't find classes that are at the high level that I need them to be at. They're too easy and I want to feel like I'm still challenged to make it worth it for me." The dancers showed a preference for physically challenging classes that provided opportunities to build their skills. Amanda felt that working hard made class more fun: "I find when I'm working at something, I tend to enjoy it more the better I'm getting at it, and have a better attitude to work harder and get better at it."

Kolb and Kalogeropoulou (2012) indicate that disciplined training and being challenged provide the framework for achievement and progression in recreational ballet class. This leads to further enjoyment and feelings of success. In my study, Karen similarly talked about mastering a skill or technique in contemporary dance: "I actually think that's one of my favourite things about dance is mastering skill...I really enjoy that part...Your body and mind is [sic] engaged in the process and makes [sic] you feel amazing after." The experience of skill mastery and success derived from commitment: hard work was rewarding as a payoff for time and effort that then fueled further work. Blair pinpointed the influence of achievement in her contemporary dance training: "It's a motivation and gives you determination, keeps you going for accomplishing just the small things. It makes you set personal goals to get that achievement...It makes you feel good about yourself too and it's like your hard work paid off."

Positive Experiences Related to Contemporary Dance Identity

The opportunity to continue dancing in a positively challenging environment was important for my interviewees. Most of the dancers had been involved in ballet since their childhood—some began to take dance classes as young as two or three years old. While the participants began with ballet in a dance studio setting, the studios did not typically offer a wide variety of adult classes, or the dancers moved to study in a different area. Several of them were introduced to contemporary dance for the first time at the university where their dance group offered an opportunity to continue dance at the high technical level to which they aspired in ballet. Not all dancers, however, came across such an opportunity without difficulty. Danielle, for example, found it difficult to find a suitable place to continue her dance career once she left her ballet studies at the studio. The other dancers were also concerned about the accessibility, skill level, and available peer groups in their local recreational dance community. Sara, Karen, and Jamie all thought finding a dance group with dancers close to their own age and level of dance training was important but challenging. While enjoying her contemporary dance company, Amanda was concerned with the accessibility and awareness of recreational dance opportunities for other dancers. She explained,

> You don't have to stop dancing just because you're not making it a profession. I think that deters a lot of people that think, "I'm not going to continue with it, I'm not looking for a career, it was just a 'for fun' thing for after school." And they don't think that can still be. They can still do it recreationally but throughout their adult life...a lot of people don't really see it that way. I think it's a lot of dance for kids and then you either stop dancing or you do it professionally.

Opening ballet dancers' minds to the diversity of recreational dance opportunities can help these dancers find opportunities to continue participation throughout the stages of their lives in the activity that they love. Having such opportunities available was particularly important because dance constituted a very central aspect of their identity.

Identification as a dancer played an important role in the interviewees' dance participation. "I have an identity as a dancer. It's a big part of my life still...I've always loved doing it and I hope to continue doing it, so definitely it's been a really positive experience for me," Jamie reflected. They were dancers: this was a part of who they were and how they lived their lives. An identity as a dancer also drove their continued involvement in contemporary dance. Amanda explained, "Why would I stop doing something that brings so much joy to my life and that has taught me so much over the years so it has become a part of me. Like I don't just say I dance, I say I'm a dancer; that's part of my identity. So that's my motivation, to say it is a part of me. I can't give up on it." Similar to the dancers in Stinson, Blumenfield-Jones, and Van Dyke's (1990) and Bracey's (2004) studies, my interviewees perceived leaving dance as unimaginable. Karen, who previously focused entirely on ballet, described her internal desire to dance as "a little voice that's just like, you miss dance, you should dance, that's kind of the biggest thing...not dancing and realizing that I don't feel complete." In dance, Sara explained, "I feel like myself. I feel very comfortable. I feel the way I should be in dance class, just, I guess, it's natural." Dancers' responses showed how participating in contemporary dance class can allow dancers with a ballet background to feel true to themselves.

My participants, echoing previous research (Bond & Stinson, 2007; Pickard & Bailey, 2009; Stinson et al., 1990), defined dance training an important site for developing determination, building self-confidence, and self-discipline. For example, Sara's life skills were influenced by her dance experience: "I like that there's [sic] so many skills you learn in dance class that are transferrable to other aspects of your life...When I was young, it taught me huge things around responsibility, things like time management...accountability." While training in class helped many of the dancers to feel more confident, they also felt more assertive in their daily lives. Chloe explained, "I think that dance has made me a lot more confident and I think that it has shaped my character, definitely." They had always felt self-assured during their previous training.

Many of my interviewees spoke about having to overcome rejection during auditions in which they had all participated when training in the studio environment. Karen, for example, recounted a childhood experience at auditions as "total rejection," and Sara described auditions as "discouraging." Danielle, who came to the dance group from a pre-professional ballet-training program, talked about the challenges of finding an outlet of dance after failed auditions: "You have these experiences and you are a dancer in your own mind, right, and it doesn't matter that anyone thinks you're not good enough. It's just an unfortunate, like where do you go now? When you want to continue your love of dance but you don't want to do it like a profession." Through auditions, Danielle began to realize that a professional career was not necessarily an option for her. She, nevertheless, was reluctant to give up dance entirely or accept that she was "not good enough." Similar to ballet dancers in Pickard and Bailey's (2009) study, Danielle and the other dancers in my study turned such rejections into opportunities to learn, inspiration to work harder, and even as indicators of future success. Amanda explained, "Every time you face a challenge you have to overcome it...Try and [sic] overcome it the best you can because that's what's going to push you forward...That's why I've had so many good experiences." Sara "reframed" her process of dealing with rejection by deciding that her "love for dance was more important than letting people tell me that I could or couldn't dance." By reframing negative occurrences, the interviewees were able to focus on their overall enjoyment of dance: "I think the good experiences outweigh the bad experiences by far...For me, most of the bad experiences and issues are kind of dependent on my response to things, so yeah, the positive experiences outweigh the bad ones" (Karen). The recreational, contemporary dance environment continued to provide positive experiences for these dancers.

The Recreational Contemporary Dance Environment

Because the dancers had now transitioned to a new environment of recreational, contemporary dance, they discussed how factors such as instructors, style of dance training, class settings, and fellow dancers made their current dance participation a positive experience.

The recreational dance setting was the site of many positive experiences and highly beneficial to my interviewees' continued participation in dance training. Jamie described her dance group: "I feel like it's...people who have been dancing their whole lives who just want to keep doing it for exercise, for fun and really enjoy doing it." Dancing for fun through recreational participation was an important aspect of their current dance training. Emily said, "It's the class style I find...keeps it sort of relaxed and more recreational and for fun, and you don't have to be too competitive or too serious." Jamie commented on the group of dancers in her recreational contemporary dance class: "Just sharing that experience with people who are in sort of the same situation as us, you know, they've grown up dancing and now just do it for fun and that common interest." Many drew comparisons between their previous competitive or pre-professional ballet involvement and their current recreational contemporary dance environment. For example, Karen explained, "When I was dancing when I was younger at the studio, it was very much oriented towards exams and performances...At [university dance group] those aren't necessarily the focal points for most people there. There's kind of just a different feeling...It's really diverse, really positive...I think everyone who comes [here] comes for different reasons and gets different things out of it and I really like that." Emily also found recreational dance to be less stressful than her previous competitive studio experience despite continuing to dance with "really good dancers": "I think personally that I've gotten to the point where I like to do it recreationally, do it for fun...I've come to be so much more comfortable with letting go and taking that pressure off and...I'm okay with just being at my level and fine dancing with a lot of really good dancers."

The social aspect of dance training was very important: sharing the in-class experience and moving with a group of other dancers was part of what made dance enjoyable. As Sara remarked of her experience, "I don't think I'd be in dance if it was just me doing it solo...I like that you work together as a group to create something and to create something that you wouldn't be able to create on your own." Gardner, Komesaroff, and Fensham (2008) found that dance participation was an important means for creating and exploring social and community values such as being comfortable physically and emotionally within a group, creating intimacy, and developing community solidarity. "I think," Danielle said, "my most positive experience in [my current] dance is the supportive environment it brings out in people, and I think people really struggle together and learn together and support each other and want to see each other succeed." Chloe explained her networking interactions within her dance group: "There's [sic] so many girls that I dance with here and they are so successful...so smart and so talented...How could you not be drawn to...get to know them more...now that we have shared dance connection?" Although training at a high skill level was important, having a social experience in class encouraged continued dance participation. Blair shared this outlook: "I most look forward to being there with my friends and people I know, not always just the dance, but I look forward to seeing people I know and my good friends at dance class."

The teaching style and personality of the instructor played a role in the dancers' current positive training experiences. Many of the interviewed dancers preferred the collaborative teaching style of their current contemporary classes; as adult dancers they wished to be treated as equals by their instructors. Drawing from her studio experience, Amanda explained how poor teaching could negatively impact class:

> [The instructor had] always been really positive and really enthused and all about loving dance and I think it was that we all started to get really good, and she just got caught up in that...She was a perfectionist...Her eye went to people who weren't trying as hard...who weren't as motivated...They weren't as serious...as the rest of us were. And she really started to pick on them... and so that really got to me. And then I heard that a lot of them were not going to be continuing the next year...I had to question, why am I here? How much do I really support my instructor?

Amanda then detailed the collaborative approach to class: "I prefer the style that is demanding but not overpowering, you know. I like my instructors to be on a level with their students, to not try to be too authoritative, especially as adults." Blair, like most participants, preferred teachers who were more relaxed and personable: "I like instructors who will talk to you about dance as well as other things and joke around, not teachers who are overly strict and just like to yell stuff out at you." Similar to Bracey's (2004) work, university dancers believed the instructor's expectations were important but also that the instructor was a person, not solely an expert and beyond reproach.

Dancers desired and appreciated the feedback, corrections, and challenges presented by their contemporary dance instructors. Bracey (2004) and Alter (1997) both found that university student dancers respect good instruction and seek constructive feedback that allows them to explore new ideas, improve, and find common ground between a teacher's standards and their own. My participants expressed similar preferences when dancing at a recreational level. For example, Karen described feedback in her classes: "I think that feedback's really important...even though we're not all going on to dance at a professional level...I think evaluating people's time and energy is really important...They're appreciating my effort even if I'm not doing something right." The instructors were also important role models to my participants. Chloe found her instructor inspirational and motivational: "She really challenges herself and you can tell...She's also pushing herself and it pushes us and motivates us to be just like her." While the participants considered the current teachers a motivation, they also had long-term meaningful relationships with their previous ballet teachers who they viewed as continual sources of mentorship and inspiration.

Conclusion

All of my interviewees continued with contemporary dance rather than ballet. Most had not been introduced to contemporary dance before attending their current dance classes, but found dancing in this recreational environment a very positive physical experience equally challenging to ballet. The three main themes—positive physical experiences, positive experiences related to dance identity, and the recreational dance environment—were important contributors to the positive experiences in dance. The emotional connection to movement provided the positive physical experience that inspired many of the ballet dancers to look for opportunities to continue dancing. The physical practice of contemporary dance then cemented their identities as dancers, which they defined as a central aspect of their lives. In addition, addressing challenges of transitioning to a new form of dance participation was considered helpful. For example, even if the dancers successfully transitioned from ballet to contemporary dance, dancing at an appropriate skill level seemed to be the most important factor to encouraging further participation.

From the phenomenological perspective, moving bodies are central to the experience of dance and the understanding of dance as a way of knowing (Fraleigh, 2000). Being physical was also central to my participants' positive experiences in my study and provided them with deepened knowledge of themselves and the cultural context of dance. "Moving for pleasure" was evident in their physicality, identity, and involvement in recreational contemporary dance and further constituted the dancers' positive experiences, challenges, and continued participation in dance. As Merce Cunningham, an influential and renowned modern dancer and choreographer, said, "You have to love dancing to stick to it. It gives you nothing back, no manuscripts to store away, no paintings to show on walls and maybe hang in museums, no poems to be printed and sold, nothing but that single fleeting moment when you feel alive" (Merce Cunningham obituary, 2009, 150). I believe that those fleeting moments of emotion and positive experiences in dance training have cemented a relationship with dance that can keep dancers active throughout their lives.

Based on their previous experiences, the dancers shared similar challenges and looked for similar ideal conditions for continued dance training. It was clear that the dancers highly valued the opportunity to dance within the university-based dance group and recognized it as an opportunity now available for many other dancers. Dancers believed that the provision of more recreational dance opportunities at an appropriate skill level would encourage adult dancers to continue. They believed that making these opportunities widely known to ballet dancers transitioning from studios or other programs and making them financially accessible could reduce barriers to continue with contemporary dance. In addition, addressing the challenges of transitioning to a new form of dance participation, broadening ballet dancers' views of the spectrum of dance opportunities, was considered critical. The dancers acknowledged that changing from vocational or pre-professional ballet training to recreational contemporary dance threatened their identities as dancers. This could be a difficult experience. However, meaningful recreational dance opportunities at the appropriate skill level eased the transition and made continued participation in new groups more enjoyable. Therefore, dance studios, schools, and other programs should be informed of the training opportunities at the recreational setting for dancers who are unable to continue at the studios. These steps may encourage all women to continue dancing, and although perseverance, drive, passion, and commitment will surely vary among dancers, those who do continue are likely to experience the joy, pleasure, and fun of dance through positive experiences in recreational dance training.

References

Aalten, A. (2005). In the presence of the body: Theorizing training, injuries and pain in ballet. *Dance Research Journal, 37*(2), 55–72.

Alexias, G., & Dimitropoulou, E. (2011). The body as a tool: Professional classical ballet dancers' embodiment. *Research in Dance Education, 12,* 87–104. doi:10.108 0/14647893.2011.575221

Allen-Collinson, J. (2009). Sporting embodiment: Sports studies and the (continuing) promise of phenomenology. *Qualitative Research in Sport and Exercise, 1,* 279–96.

Alter, J. B. (1997). Why dance students pursue dance: Studies of dance students from 1953 to 1993. *Dance Research Journal, 29*(2), 70–89.

Andrzejewski, C. E. (2009). Toward a model of holistic dance teacher education. *Journal of Dance Education, 9,* 17–26.

Benn, T., & Walters, D. (2001). Between Scylla and Charybdis: Nutritional education versus body culture and the ballet aesthetic: The effects on the lives of female dancers. *Research in Dance Education, 2,* 139–54. doi:10.1080/14647890120100773

Bond, K. E., & Stinson, S. W. (2007). "It's work, work, work, work": Young people's experiences of effort and engagement in dance. *Research in Dance Education, 8,* 155–83. doi:10.1080/14647890701706115

Bracey, L. (2004). Voicing connections: An interpretive study of dancers' experiences. *Research in Dance Education, 5,* 7–24. doi:10.1080/14647890420001 90852

Burgess, G., Grogan, S., & Burwitz, L. (2006). Effects of a 6-week aerobic dance intervention on body image and physical self-perceptions in adolescent girls. *Body Image, 3,* 57–66. doi:10.1016/j.bodyim.2005.10.005

de Bruin, A. P., Bakker, F. C., & Oudejans, R. R. D. (2009). Achievement goal theory and disordered eating: Relationships of disordered eating with goal orientations and motivational climate in female gymnasts and dancers. *Psychology of Sport and Exercise, 10,* 72–79. doi:10.1016/j.psychsport.2008.07.002

Dryburgh, A., & Fortin S. (2010). Weighing in on surveillance: Perception of the impact of surveillance on female ballet dancers' health. *Research in Dance Education, 11,* 95–108. doi:10.1080/14647893.2010.482979

Dyer, B. (2010). The perils, privileges and pleasures of seeking right from wrong: Reflecting upon student perspectives of social processes, value systems, agency and the becoming of identity in the dance technique classroom. *Research in Dance Education, 11,* 109–29. doi:10.1080/14647893.2010.482978

Fraleigh, S. (2000). Consciousness matters. *Dance Research Journal, 32*(1), 54–66.

Fisher, J. (2007). Tulle as tool: Embracing the conflict of the ballerina as powerhouse. *Dance Research Journal, 39*(1), 2–24

Gardner, S. M., Komesaroff, P., & Fensham, R. (2008). Dancing beyond exercise: Young people's experiences in dance classes. *Journal of Youth Studies, 11,* 701–09. doi:10.1080/13676260802393294

Giorgi, A. (1975). An application of phenomenological method in psychology. In A. Giorgi, C. Fisher, & E. Murray (Eds.), *Duquesne studies in phenomenological psychology* (Vol. 2) (82–103). Pittsburgh, PA: Duquesne University Press.

Gray, K.M., & Kunkel, M.A. (2001). The experience of female ballet dancers: A grounded theory. *High Ability Studies, 12,* 7–25. doi:10.1080/13598130125382

Green, J. (2001). Socially constructed bodies in American dance classrooms. *Research in Dance Education, 2,* 155–73. doi:10.1080/14647890120100782

Huddy, A., & Stevens, K. (2011). The teaching artist: A model for university dance teacher training. *Research in Dance Education, 12,* 157–71.

Jackson, J. (2005). My dance and the ideal body: Looking at ballet practice from the inside out. *Research in Dance Education, 6,* 25–40. doi:10.1080/14617890500373089

Kolb, A., & Kalogeropoulou, S. (2012). In defence of ballet: Women, agency and the philosophy of pleasure. *Dance Research, 30,* 107–25. doi:10.3366/drs.2012.0042

Kvale, S. & Brinkmann, S. (2009). *Interviews: Learning the craft of qualitative research interviewing* (2nd ed.). Thousand Oaks, CA: Sage.

Kvale S. & Brinkmann S. (2007). *Interviews: Learning the craft of qualitative research interviewing.* London: Sage.

Lewis, R. N., & Scannell, E. D. (1995). Relationship of body image and creative dance movement. *Perceptual Motor Skill, 81,* 155–60.

Mainwaring, L. M., & Krasnow, D. H. (2010). Teaching the dance class: Strategies to enhance skill acquisition, mastery and positive self-image. *Journal of Dance Education, 10,* 14–21.

Markula, P., & Silk, M. (2011). *Qualitative research for physical culture.* Basingstoke, UK: Palgrave Macmillan.

McEwen, K., & Young, K. (2011). Ballet and pain: Reflections on a risk-dance culture. *Qualitative Research in Sport, Exercise & Health, 3*(2), 152–73.

Merce Cunningham obituary. (2009, December). *Time, 174*(25), 150.

Nordin-Bates, S. M., Walker, I. J., & Redding, E. (2011). Correlates of disordered eating attitudes among male and female young talented dancers: Findings from the UK centres for advanced training. *Eating Disorders, 19*, 211–33.

Parviainen, J. (2002). Bodily knowledge: Epistemological reflections on dance. *Dance Research Journal, 34*(1), 11–26.

Penniment, K. J., & Egan, S. J. (2010). Perfectionism and learning experiences in dance class as risk factors for eating disorders in dancers. *European Eating Disorders Review, 20*, 13–22.

Pickard, A. (2012). Schooling the dancer: The evolution of an identity as a ballet dancer. *Research in Dance Education, 13*, 25–46. doi:10.1080/14647893.2011.6511 19

Pickard, A., & Bailey, R. (2009). Crystallising experiences among young elite dancers. *Sport, Education and Society, 14*(2), 165–81.

Rouhiainen, L. (2008). Somatic dance as a means of cultivating ethically embodied subjects. *Research in Dance, 9*, 241–56. doi:10.1080/14647890802386916

Stinson, S. W., Blumenfield-Jones, D., & Van Dyke, J. (1990). Voices of young women dance students: An interpretive study of meaning in dance. *Dance Research Journal, 22* (2): 13–22.

Thomas, H., & Tarr, J. (2009). Dancers' perceptions of pain and injury: Positive and negative effects. *Journal of Dance Medicine & Science, 13*, 51–59.

Turner, B. S., & Wainwright, S. P. (2003). Corps de ballet: The case of the injured ballet dancer. *Sociology of Health & Illness, 25*, 269–88.

Vertinsky, P. (2010). From physical educators to mothers of the dance: Margaret H'Doubler and Martha Hill. *The International Journal for the History of Sport, 27*, 1113–32.

Wainwright, S. P., & Turner, B. S. (2004). Epiphanies of embodiment: Injury, identity and the balletic body. *Qualitative Research, 4*, 311–37.

Walker, I. J., & Nordin-Bates, S. M. (2010). Performance anxiety experiences of professional ballet dancers: The importance of control. *Journal of Dance Medicine & Science, 14*(4), 133–45.

Appendix: Participant Demographics

Participant	Age	Years of dance participation	University relationship	Previous dance training	Occupation
Amanda	19	16	Student	Ballet, tap, jazz, lyrical, hip hop, modern, musical theatre	Student
Blair	18	14	Student	Ballet, jazz, modern	Student
Chloe	23	15	Community	Ballet, jazz, tap, musical theatre, lyrical, modern, contemporary	Business administrator
Danielle	22	10	Community	Contemporary, ballet, jazz	Office worker
Emily	26	24	Alumni	Ballet, jazz	Office worker
Jamie	28	24	Alumni	Ballet, jazz, musical theatre, lyrical, modern	Physical education consultant
Karen	36	20	Student	Ballet	Academic
Sara	30	26	Staff	Ballet, jazz, tap, modern, lyrical	Social worker

6

AT THE BARRE

Ethical Training for Beginner Ballet Class

Jodie Vandekerkhove

I begin with my story. The small, thin dancer with her hair pulled back into a bun, her pink tights and bodysuit on, walks into the space and looks sheepishly at the ballet barres placed in the middle of the floor for the start of a beginner ballet class. She is obviously checking her body out in the mirrors, deciding whether she looks the part. Timid, scared, and unsure of her surroundings, without saying a word she walks to the ballet barre. Trying to feel like she belongs, she starts stretching with her leg up at the barre; she is obviously in pain. I am walking deliberately around in the space. They observe me, a six-foot tall woman wearing long black leggings with a sweatshirt covering my arms. I ask, "Is everyone OK?" No one says a peep; I sense the silence and the bodies in the space. They just want to be told what to do and how to do it, because that is what ballet dancers do. We begin with the pliés. I sense the relief among the dancers. They are now all dancing amongst the entire group learning ballet for the first time. Class has commenced.

Recreational ballet is exceptionally popular: young girls attend dance studios and adult women's ballet classes frequently fill up (Kolb & Kalogeropoulou, 2012). As a testimony to this trend, the beginner ballet classes offered by Campus and Community Recreation at the University of Alberta are frequently fully subscribed. I presently instruct several such ballet classes, and through my own experiences as a ballet teacher, I became interested in studying the experiences of beginner recreational ballet dancers.

As an instructor, I have observed that many beginner dancers are uncomfortable in their new surroundings and seem quite reserved. Because of this, I was inspired to examine how ballet is taught. In this chapter, I detail my research project that focused on beginner ballet dancers' and their instructor's experiences in one class. I first review previous literature on ballet instruction and then explain my theoretical framework, which draws on the work of Michel Foucault, particularly his concept of disciplinary techniques. I then discuss the methods I used to collect data before presenting my findings. To conclude, I present suggestions for future research in ballet training.

Production of Docile Bodies in Ballet

Previous scholarly work has highlighted many problems in the practice of ballet, including high injury rates (Aalten, 1995; Dryburgh & Fortin, 2010; Garrich & Reque, 1993; Kolb & Kalogeropoulou, 2012; Turner & Wainwright, 2003; Wainwright & Turner, 2004) and body image problems resulting from the ideal, thin, and hyperflexible ballerina's body (Anshel, 2004; Benn & Walters, 2001; Bettle, Bettle, Neumarker, & Neumarker, 2001; Ravaldi et al., 2006; Tiggemann & Slater, 2001). As a result, there have also been some suggestions for providing safer ballet training.

According to Barr and Risner (2014), previous research on teaching ballet can be divided into two strands. The individual model focuses on improving individual teacher's teaching methods in a ballet class. The social model, instead, aims to account for the social context for dance teaching. Following the principles of critical pedagogy (e.g., Barr & Risner, 2014; Shapiro, 1998), these scholars use dance as an emancipatory practice that can raise consciousness of inequality in the world in general. Although both models can provide fruitful foundations for improving ballet training, in my project I was interested in how an individual ballet teacher's practices might embed, even if not intentionally, disciplinary practices. Therefore, I am interested in teaching practices, but instead of seeing ballet as a means for raising consciousness of social problems, my focus is on how ballet training itself might act as a powerful disciplinary tool. Therefore, departing from both the individual and social models, in this literature review, I draw upon Foucault's understanding of docile bodies, discipline, power, and the body to understand how a typical ballet class is organized and what type of dancers it produces. I examine the previous literature on ballet through the mechanisms of time, space, and movement based on Foucault's theory of disciplinary techniques. Although Foucault never wrote about dance or, more specifically, ballet, he did focus on the disciplinary body techniques that create docile bodies. His concepts can aid in understanding students' ballet experiences and how the environment of the ballet class shapes their bodies. Other scholars (e.g., Green, 2003; Ritenburg, 2010) have also used Foucault's insights to examine dance training. In my review, I have incorporated their findings in my discussion of Foucault's disciplinary techniques.

Ballet has become popular for its poise, balance, elegance, and flexibility, but there are also unintended consequences of ballet training that can lead to the production of unthinking docile bodies. It is important to highlight how dominant social reality shapes ballet while also focusing on "the ways an intendedly liberatory pedagogy might function as part of the technology of surveillance, examination and normalization" (Fraleigh & Hanstein, 1999, 111). Foucault (1995) had a great interest in how power operates through the mechanisms of time, space, and movement, with the end result, he claimed, of disciplining the body into docility. I now discuss Foucault's disciplinary techniques—the use of space, time, and movement—and how they can operate in a ballet class to further understand how ballet bodies turn into docile bodies.

Space

Disciplinary space is distributed in a certain manner to increase bodily discipline or, as Foucault (1995) suggests, discipline engages the art of distribution. There are various characteristics of space that discipline bodies, including ballet bodies: the enclosure, partitioning, functionality, and the use of rank within the space. First, ballet studios are set up as large rooms with closed doors, very few windows, and often no natural light in their enclosure. Ballet class requires the enclosure of space, the use of the mirrors and ballet barres, and ballet-specific clothing that reveals the joints and lines of the body. Mirrors have long been used as teaching tools in ballet instruction and have proven to be a potent element in affecting the dancers' body image. For example, Green (1999) found that university dance students' use of mirrors intensified their sense of objective self-awareness through which they learned to view themselves as objects. Ultimately, these dancers perceived a negative influence with the presence of the mirrors, which resulted in physical self-evaluation, behaviour regulation, body objectification, and competition.

Second, the ballet studio is partitioned: the dancers are usually organized in lines within the dance studio space to be visible to the instructor throughout the class. Often, these dancers are arranged in lines or at the barre, where they are on display wearing tight-fitting clothing. Such spacing encourages the dancers to constantly check how they fit in with the rest of the dancers. The use of the mirrors and approval from the instructor creates a sense of hierarchical observation. As Atencio and Wright (2009) suggest, "spaces are constructed by and constitutive of social identities, practices, and power relations" (33). In this space, the dance instructor is in a position of power, providing guidance, observation, and supervision for the other bodies in the space, and thus becomes a part of the mechanism through which the ballet bodies are disciplined. To summarize, the ballet studio space creates a mechanism of control through the hierarchal observation enabled by the partitioned space (Foucault, 1995).

Third, typical ballet studio space is functional and useful. The dancers view their bodies from the mirrors on the walls. Ballet barres are attached to the sides of the wall. Together, these elements create a functional space for its specific purpose: dance teaching. The ballet dancers often learn their information and vocabulary by mimicking the teacher in the space (Whittier, 2006): they learn the proper execution of the steps as a unified group. Through the use of functional space, as Green (2003) suggests, practicing ballet becomes normative. Normative refers to what is learned and accepted as the correct use of the space when learning the movement. For example, the students learn the instructor should be positioned at the front of the room to be visible to the dancers. As suggested earlier, according to Foucault (1995), this arrangement ranks the teacher over the dancers, who then come to regard the teacher's surveillance, observation, and supervision as normal.

Finally, the dancers place themselves within the studio space based on their individual ranks. In the ballet studio, the technically most proficient dancer is placed in the front centre of the room or at the end of the barre so that the other dancers can easily view her as an example to follow. Although not often officially acknowledged, all the dancers are aware of the hierarchical ranking of different spaces in the studio. The ranking of the dancers within the space then becomes normal ballet practice.

Time

The second aspect I discuss is the use of time in a ballet class. Foucault (1995) describes how use of time comes to control activities in the enclosed space. Ballet technique classes are provided on a weekly schedule with particular focus on a number of repeated exercises that incorporate codified steps using specified tempos, rhythms, and body positions. Foucault (1995) suggests that time, because it provides a new set of restraints, brings another degree of precision in the breakdown of movements—"another way of adjusting the body to temporal imperatives" (151). The dancers push through pain to keep up with the tempo or timing of the movements to achieve technical proficiency required in classical ballet (Ritenburg, 2010). Due the high technical requirements, ballet class requires a very strong discipline from its participants.

Foucault (1995) reminds us that "time penetrates the body and with it all the meticulous controls of power to render a subject docile" (152). In ballet class, the time penetrates the dancer's body through exercises learned in unison. According to McEwen and Young (2011), ballet stems from a militaristic and controlling social institution; accordingly, in ballet classes the individual dancers learn how to "articulate" as a group. As a result, "the individual [ballet] body becomes a unit within a mass" (74). The group learns to perform without any adjustment of tempo to accommodate the different bodies in the space. For example, dancers need to place their heels on the ground when landing jumps to avoid injuries. This safety measure, however, becomes impossible when the footwork is frequently performed at a very fast tempo (Kolb & Kalogeropoulou, 2012). Dancers seldom question these types of requirements, and thus become what Foucault would call docile bodies—bodies that unquestioningly follow the instructions to perform ballet movements efficiently. This way, a certain type of training is assumed to be "correct training" that is never questioned. It also becomes normal practice that is further verified as the correct way of training in ballet by the instructor who determines which exercises are included in the class and how they are executed. Thus, in ballet, a certain stylized way of moving is normalized as the correct technique.

The correct timing of ballet technique is achieved by following the music and the instructor's advice on what is considered normal performance. Consequently, the music controls the time and becomes part of the mechanism that controls the dancers' bodies. Ballet dancers are often pushed to achieve impeccable technical skills that require a clear acquisition of timing in each exercise (Whittier, 2006). In a ballet class, a set amount of time for the barre and centre work is clearly specified through precise timing, rhythm, and tempo for each exercise. In addition, repetition of monotonous practices (Foucault, 1995) is a tool utilized frequently in a ballet class. Each exercise is repeated until it is executed correctly, efficiently, and at the proper speed. As Franko (2011) observes, "disciplinary control does not consist simply in teaching or imposing a series of particular gestures; it imposes the best relation between a gesture and the overall position of the body, which is its condition of efficiency and speed" (99). Therefore, the correct use of time in a ballet class plays a critical role in determining which dancers are ranked as successful. The normative timing, however, does not consider the structures of different bodies, but determines productive use and control of the series of movements (Foucault, 1995) for the normal ballet body. Therefore, the use of time is a way to institute a sense of power and control over learning the specific ballet movements.

Movement

Foucault (1995) explains that controlled movement needs to be organized efficiently. In ballet class, the movement material is organized in a very exact manner to produce ballet bodies that move in an elegant way with precision (Ritenburg, 2010). Ballet, thus, has developed its own, detailed movement language. Foucault notes, "A whole analytical pedagogy was being formed, meticulous in its detail" (159). Although Foucault does not discuss the particular pedagogy of ballet, one can examine what meticulous details are emphasized when teaching ballet.

The efficient organization of movement becomes a disciplinary technique when it is used to produce docile bodies moving in the space in a uniform manner. Ballet is often credited to require the highest level of technical skill of all the different dance genres. As such, it is designed to produce bodies moving seamlessly as a group.

The language of learning the ballet movements is immersed in the ballet culture: "In order for ballet dancers to reproduce ballet technique and choreography with precision and clarity, they must understand the whole language of the technique—the steps, the methods of executing the steps, the shapes and lines of the positions, the sequencing of the class and the exercises, and the style or aesthetic of the movements" (Whittier, 2006, 126). Although ballet has created its own movement vocabulary, the basic elements of ballet movement provide general training in strength and skill. Movement in a ballet class incorporates a strong use of codified steps that make up sequences of movement. This type of organization of the movements in a ballet class enables the dancers to learn the technique effectively, but can also create unintended consequences. For example, Ritenburg (2010) suggests that when ballet teachers force everybody into the idealized ballet body, the result could be physical and psychological damage. For instance, a forced turn-out position that a dancer's body cannot anatomically hold can damage her body. Forcing the different bodies in each class into shapes and positions that are not anatomically possible is detrimental. Ballet teachers and instructors need to be mindful of the dangers of ballet technique. In a sense, as Green (1999) suggests, dance students give their bodies to their teachers. Following Foucault (1995), however, these dancers turn into docile bodies if they are not taught to question the use of the many taken-for-granted ballet exercises. Many ballet dancers strive for perfection when executing specific ballet exercises without considering the health of their bodies. Following Foucault (1995), therefore, ballet dancers aim to become normal ballet bodies by perfecting their technique and being "like everyone else" in the class. This process normalizes their individual bodies into the accepted ballet aesthetic. The ballet movement, consequently, remains an important aspect of how we know about ballet, and thus, as Hamera (2005) states, rewrites "bodies' and communities' relationships to space, to time, and to the intersections of both" (93).

Participant	Years of dance participation	Previous dance training	Education
Addison	2	ballet	Fourth-year undergraduate
Amy	2	ballet	Third-year undergraduate
Lee	2	ballet	Graduate (master of arts)
Michelle	none	none	First-year undergraduate
Cindy (instructor)	24	• ballet and contemporary dance • 24 years of professional experience as a teacher, dancer, and choreographer	• Bachelor of physical education • Dance performance diploma • Dance teacher-training diploma • Royal Academy of Dancing ballet certification • Certified Pilates mat instructor

Several scholars use a Foucauldian perspective to conclude that ballet training produces docile bodies. For example, Ritenburg (2010) demonstrates that the structure of a ballet class is strictly organized for maximum efficiency towards building a functional dancing body. She also examines ballet teachers' roles in dance education to argue that they tend to train their students effectively as a mass of bodies using the control of the space, the control of the activity, and the exhaustive use of the body through complex movements that require the acquisition of knowledge (Ritenberg, 2010). She concludes that such mechanisms of power clearly operate in ballet training to produce docile bodies. Along with Ritenberg (2010), Green (2003) discusses how dance training is an oppressive practice that requires the subjects (dancers) to be surveyed and corrected in dance technique classes. Green (2003) claims, "Student dance bodies are docile bodies created to produce efficiency, not only of movement, but also, a normalization and standardization of behavior in dance classes" (100).

In summary, ballet training appears to create the docile bodies through the disciplinary use of space, time, and movement vocabulary. Based on a Foucauldian reading, then, it may be tempting to conclude that it might be best to simply abandon ballet. Ballet, however, is still very popular among many women who sincerely enjoy dance (Kolb & Kalogeropoulou, 2012). Thus, the answer is not simply to forget ballet but to consider how to make its practices better. Given that most ballet experiences start with a beginner recreational ballet class, I am interested in whether this class is necessarily a disciplinary practice. More specifically, I ask, how do space, time, and movement operate within a beginner ballet class?

Methodology

In my research, I used qualitative methodology to examine ballet training. More particularly, I approached ballet from a poststructuralist, Foucauldian perspective to analyze the disciplinarity of a typical ballet class. The qualitative research methods that focus on subjective experiences and knowledge-making are suitable for examinations like my research, which explores how individual ballet dancers view their training. Previous dance researchers define dance as qualitatively constituted. For example, Fraleigh and Hanstein (1999) state, "Dance is qualitatively constituted in movement and experience" (8). Poststructuralism refers to a research paradigm that acknowledges "that language powerfully structures social meanings, power relations and individual consciousness" (Markula & Silk, 2011, 49). Foucauldian poststructuralism locates bodily practices, such as ballet training, within a larger social context of power relations and knowledge production. I solicited the dancers' and their teacher's individual feelings, experiences, and knowledges of a beginner ballet class through the qualitative interviewing process to uncover answers to my research question (Markula & Silk, 2011). More detailed descriptions about each participant are included in Table 6.1.

Markula and Silk (2011) remind us that interviews are conversations with a purpose. My purpose was to examine how space, time, and movement operated within a beginner ballet class and how the dancers and their teacher perceived them. I selected four dancers and their instructor for semi-structured interviews (Markula & Silk, 2011) from a beginners' ballet class. These participants were easily accessible to me through the previous contacts I had gained as a ballet teacher. My interview guide was based on Foucault's disciplinary techniques. I asked my participants to reflect upon the use of time, space, and movement practices in a typical beginner ballet class. The typical length of an interview was one hour, which allowed me to obtain in-depth information about each participant's experiences. Before conducting my interviews I obtained ethics approval from the University of Alberta Research Ethics Board. I analyzed my interviews using my insights from Foucauldian theory. From the poststructuralist perspective, my work emphasized the theoretical contributions and the impact on the community I was researching (Markula & Silk, 2011). Thus, I used my theoretical perspective as a guide to provide coherence throughout my work.

The Use of Time, Space, and Movement in a Beginner's Ballet Class

My interviews provided insights into how the participants and their teacher viewed a typical beginner ballet class. Although my analysis revealed several themes, I have organized my discussion here based on the participants' conceptualizations of their class space, how it was timed, and what ballet exercises were performed in a typical class.

The "Multipurpose" Ballet Space

Based on their descriptions, my participants' ballet space represented a standard ballet space (Ritenburg, 2010): ballet barres and mirrors lined the walls; there was a wooden floor; and the studio was a large, open space. Their ballet class, however, was taught in a "very, very big" gymnasium (Lee) that Addison described as a "multipurpose" room with "a lot of room for travelling and floor work" (Amy). It was so large that some participants found it "overwhelming" (Michelle). Similar to the dancers, Cindy, the instructor, described the space as a "very large space, too big," but also noted that it did accommodate a large class. Because it was a multipurpose space, the dancers noted, it was not always clean.

All participants recognized the ballet barre was the part of the room in which they spent most of their class time. Similar to Ritenburg (2010), they discussed the standardized functions of the different spaces within the room—the barre versus "the centre"—and the typical structure this created for their class. The primary purpose for using the barre was warming up the body (Amy, Addison). In addition, the participants defined the barre as a space that created stability, balance, and support. It was also space for stretching. Similar to dancers in McEwen and Young's (2011) study, my participants recognized the conventional structure of the ballet class where emphasis is placed on "hours of repetitive barre exercises" (153). Addison, nevertheless, suggested, "I think there is a discipline to starting at the barre." Interestingly, she openly referred to "discipline," which Foucault (1995) understands to create docile but functional bodies through a certain use of space.

According to my participants, the ballet space was created for visibility, particularly through the use of mirrors. Previous research has debated the benefits of mirrors when learning dance. For example, Adame, Blumenkehl, Cole, and Radell (2011) discuss how the use of mirrors might negatively influence dancers' perception, thoughts, and feelings about their bodies, resulting in a negative body image. Cindy acknowledged the positives and negatives of using the mirror as an instructional tool, stating that ballet "is an aesthetic art, but sometimes it [the mirror] can make me self-conscious, always thinking I should look a certain way." Cindy faced the mirrors when teaching the centre practice and found that using the mirrors helped the students in terms of visual cueing. Nevertheless, Cindy suggested she sometimes used mirrors out of habit rather than a necessary tool of teaching. This echoed Dryburgh and Fortin (2010), who also found that mirrors were often used out of habit. Michelle, Lee, and Amy recognized that the teacher typically has everyone facing the mirror during the centre practice so that all the dancers are visible in the mirrors. Cindy justified this practice as a chance for all dancers to see their bodies in the mirrors and, accordingly, organized the dancers in lines in front of the mirror. The dancers, however, expressed a desire to occasionally detach themselves from this habit and wanted to change the practice of facing the mirrors. For instance, they pointed out that without the mirror, they did not compare themselves to the others in the space. They also felt that is was more important to "feel" the movement than to see the body in the mirror. For example, Amy found it important to have the ability "to disconnect from the mirror and from the feeling itself and being able to recognize [her] body without having to visually examine it."

The participants remarked that the ballet space lends itself well to observation. According to Green (1999), observation in ballet space can act as a method of control that combines hierarchical observation by the teacher, the other dancers, and the dancer herself. She adds that tight-fitting clothing in a ballet class creates hypersensitive body consciousness, particularly because the dancers are required to regularly look at themselves in the mirror. Cindy found it important that the dancers wore tight-fitting clothing so that she could correct them anatomically. Michelle, Lee, and Addison, in turn, asserted that most dancers just want to be comfortable in what they wear in a ballet class, but at the same time, the clothing should not be so "baggy" that one's movement is restricted. Although these participants preferred to wear something comfortable and "non-traditional," Amy embraced the traditional attire: "A lot of people come to this class that I am in currently wearing socks but at some point I think it denotes a certain lack of dedication to it to not wear the proper shoes. At some point you need to remember we are in a class where our bodies are being examined and this is necessary." Therefore, traditional clothing, for Amy, created the full experience of dancing in a beginner ballet class. Amy was one of the participants with more ballet experience and obviously held preconceived knowledge about ballet class that she did not question. Following Foucault (1995), she seemed more disciplined into a normative ballet body than the participants with less experience.

The centre space provided more discussion regarding observation and visibility in the ballet class. In this space, the dancers performed either alone or in a group. While the participants, in general, liked dancing in a group, being with more advanced or confident dancers could feel "intimidating" (Lee) or " uncomfortable" (Michelle). Addison noticed a somewhat competitive atmosphere in these situations because they raised the level of performance standards. When instructing, Cindy preferred one group observing the dancing group while they waited their turn to perform the exercise. This demanded constant observation that, according to Foucault (1995), would increase the disciplinarity of the ballet space.

In summary, the ballet space and class structure of this beginner ballet class followed a particular spatial arrangement that allowed for high visibility and constant observation. In a Foucauldian sense, then, this beginner class can be considered "a disciplinary space" that is partitioned based on functionality (Foucault, 1995, 145). Thus, the organization of the ballet space in this study confirmed the observations by the previous researchers (Green, 1999; Ritenburg, 2010): it was a space clearly compartmentalized based on the function of ballet. The dancers, for the most part, did not question the preconceived traditional ideas of the ballet space that enabled constant hierarchical observation (Foucault, 1995). While functional, this space tended to create docile dancers.

Efficient Use of Time in the Ballet Class

If space provided the basic structure for the beginner ballet class, the efficient use of time further defined this structure. Ritenburg (2010) discusses how the specific timetable establishes control over the activity during ballet class. My findings align with her study, but my participants discussed the time spent in each space in more detail. In general, they found the ballet barre occupied the majority of class time. Michelle, Lee, Addison, and Amy believed that the time was used efficiently and did not question the structure of their ballet class. These dancers were satisfied with the quality of use of time that eliminated disturbances and distractions under constant supervision of their instructor. Although aware of the structure, some dancers, such as Michelle and Amy, lost track of time during the ballet class. For example, Amy said, "I don't know, I have never really kept track of time that way." In this sense, these dancers were not entirely docile bodies but felt that, as university students, participating in a beginner ballet class allowed them to escape from the realities of student life. Michelle saw her ballet class as a welcomed break: "I made myself sign up for something so I could guarantee that at least once a week I am just going to leave every-thing else behind."

Foucault (1995) notes that repetition produces efficiency. All the dancers noted that repetition was often employed in a begin-ner ballet class. Cindy believed that repeating ballet exercises was important for beginner dancers because it allowed the dancer's body "to take over with the muscle memory." This involved less thinking over time, and thus the use of repetition enabled the dancers' bodies to "do more." While Cindy believed that repeti-tion provided a positive way of learning ballet, it also involved less thinking, and thus allowed dancers to unquestioningly perform their exercises. In Foucauldian terms, then, repetition of ballet exercises potentially added to the docility of the dancers. The danc-ers indeed explained that repetition—it was common to have an exercise repeated two to four times—increased the efficient use of time in the class. They also used repetition to improve their perfor-mance. Addison, for example, appreciated repetition because she was "a bit of a perfectionist." For Michelle, repeating the exercises in a class gave opportunities to "try to improve the next time." Amy, however, disliked repeating exercises; she remarked, "If you repeat something it's because something was wrong with the last one." According to Foucault (1995), repetition results in constant self-surveillance in order to catch and correct any flaws, which

Amy indicated. However, it can also lead to the consequent quest to perfect one's performance, to become closer to a "normal" ballet dancer.

According to my participants, music is a critical aspect in a beginner ballet class. All my participants used the term *musicality* when describing the importance of staying in time with the music in a beginner ballet class. Addison noted that musicality is "a relationship with music and movement," and Amy added that it creates cohesiveness and co-ordination with the group of dancers. The participants obviously recognized a correlation between music and time. In addition, music created the opportunity to work seamlessly together as a group. Foucault (1995) indicates that the position of the body, limbs, an aptitude, and duration of time are all utilized to create a coherently operating group. In this type of work, "time penetrates the body and with it all the meticulous controls of power" (Foucault, 1995, 152). Therefore, the use of music can be understood to discipline dancing bodies as it provides an impetus and a strategy to dance in unison. Cindy openly stated that staying in time with the music is "just part of the discipline" of ballet, and thus a central aspect of teaching dance.

A variety of ballet exercises (specific ballet exercises usually concentrate on one or two aspects of the ballet movement) are performed at different tempos both at the barre and during the centre work. An increased tempo was a challenge to the participants. For example, Addison felt that her "body will just take short cuts and I don't actually articulate the full movement." Lee described it as "overwhelming." When a beginner ballet dancer is learning a new way to move, it needs to be simple, clear, and articulated with clear timing. When too many progressions were added, these dancers tended to feel overwhelmed. Trying to incorporate them all led to feeling less successful, which was "discouraging" (Lee). In a ballet class, learning the correct timing to work seamlessly as a group reinforces ballet as a disciplinary practice (Foucault, 1995; Ritenburg, 2010).

In summary, the correct use of time in a beginner ballet class increases efficiency. Music complements this goal as it enables the dancers to work together, at the same time. According to Foucault (1995), time efficiency increases the control of activity. My participants definitely expressed how important the proper timing of movement was in the class. In addition, the use of time in this study confirmed the observations by the previous researchers: ballet technique classes are provided on a weekly schedule with a particular focus on a number of repeated exercises that incorporate codified steps using specific timing, tempos, and rhythms (Hamera, 2005). The dancers believed that the preconceived traditional idea of the use of time in a ballet class was efficient. While this type of use of time is purposeful, it created docile dancers who did not need to question the ways ballet technique was practiced. Foucault (1995) argues that discipline creates docile bodies that function efficiently in a timely manner without questioning the process. The efficient use of time, however, was believed to create flawless, high-quality movement performance and was not questioned.

Learning Quality Ballet Movement

Learning ballet movements can often pose challenges for the participants. Participants in this beginner-level ballet class demonstrated a range of skill level. To accommodate these differences, Cindy aimed to find an individual in class who executed the movement well and used her as example for other dancers to follow. As she noted, "It makes them [the dancers] feel good that they are valued." Michelle, Lee, and Amy agreed with their instructor: this was a good "motivator" and provided "an example." Foucault (1995) might consider that singling out examples ranks the dancers, and thus works as a disciplinary technique, fostering comparison and judgements within the class. While Addison felt it was not important for her to find an "example," she acknowledged, nevertheless, that she tended to start "comparing herself to the other dancers."

Such comparisons can act as normalizing judgement (Foucault, 1995) that assesses an individual based on a standard norm to which she must measure up. The normalizing judgement also leads the dancers to monitor themselves at every stage of learning the ballet movements. Dryburgh and Fortin (2010) noted that constant surveillance is a part of dancers' learning experiences as each dancer strives to achieve a normal ballet body. Addison, who could not help measuring herself against others, seemed to have internalized the normalizing judgement.

Despite comparisons to other dancers, the quality of the movement was an important aspect that provided the dancers a way to express themselves in ballet movements. For example, Addison felt that "precision, elegance, and grace" made ballet movements ballet, while Amy recognized "form and structure" as essential qualities of ballet. It was very important for Amy to "try to embody a certain emotion or aesthetic" when she tried "to perform a movement." Qualities such as grace and elegance can also be seen to emphasize freedom and creativity, instead of discipline, when learning the ballet movements. For example, Kolb and Kalogeropoulou (2012) describe how the physicality in learning ballet movements provides the pleasure of practicing the ballet technique.

Although quality was important, according to my participants, specific technical details of the ballet exercises were emphasized when learning movements. As Ritenburg (2010) discusses, ballet technique provides the specialized knowledge for elegant ballet movements that require precision and a heightened attention to the details of movements. Paraphrasing Foucault (1995), ballet is meticulous in its detail, with precise arms, legs, and even head movements required in each exercise and combination. According to Michelle, however, learning the specific details produced "satisfaction," and Addison explained that it was important for the "expression of the movement." Amy added that the precision created "part of the cohesive movement." Lee and Addison described the attention to detail as "perfecting each movement" (Lee). Foucault (1995) explains that disciplinary practices often emphasize perfection. Hamara (2005), in turn, suggests that ballet, through its meticulous and relentless process of visual scrutiny, creates the "ideal" ballet dancer. "Ideal" refers to perfection that consequently becomes "an effect and an object of discipline" (Foucault, 1995, 161). However, attention to the details often creates a quality of correct ballet movement that the participants, similar to Kolb and Kalogeropoulou's (2012) dancers, enjoyed. Although Michelle felt that too much detail in a beginner ballet class was overwhelming, the participants expressed "joy, happiness, love, and frustration" (Lee, Addison, Michelle, and Amy) when learning to master a technical skill.

In a beginner ballet class, the role of the instructor was critical in facilitating movement choices. All dancers indicated that the teacher needed to use all of the senses when delivering the movement instruction: providing a demonstration, verbal feedback, imagery, and touch. Their instructor, Cindy, did indeed provide feedback using verbal feedback, imagery, and touching if necessary. For Addison, it was important to have the instructor facilitate the movement or correct it "within the body." In this process, the instructor became an observer of Addison's body performance, which increased the use of hierarchical observation already prevalent in ballet. In contrast, Amy preferred the instructor to point out the individual dancer who executed the movements either correctly or incorrectly. Amy even called for less demonstration and more examination in the beginner ballet class. As Ritenburg (2010) notes, the "exhaustive use of the body through exercises as tasks of the examination" (74) produces disciplinary training techniques.

Often, the instructor presented specific movements, and students anticipated her praise and attention through correction and physical manipulation. In this relationship, the instructor was often viewed as an all-knowing expert and authority (Green, 1999). Amy referred to her instructor as an expert who controlled the movements and the bodies in the space: "The teacher helps to teach the movement, guide how movement should look, and reflect the observations of what people are doing and how to correct improper posture or placement." Foucault (1995) explains how the use of expert knowledge reinforces disciplinary techniques when the expert uses her power deriving from the specific skills needed within the environment. For example, a ballet teacher becomes a disciplinary expert when teaching movements that strictly follow the traditions of ballet without problematizing their meaning.

As I indicated earlier, learning complicated ballet exercises requires practice and repetition, but also time to observe the teacher. Addison stressed the importance of "breaking each movement down" for her when learning the challenging ballet combinations. Indeed, when Cindy taught complicated, longer sequences, she did break them down into smaller segments. She worked on one section at a time and repeated it before adding more movement material to the original section, "repeating it over and over until they [the dancers] feel comfortable." She also provided progressions to challenge the students both mentally and physically. Progression referred to several aspects: doing the same movement faster, adding body parts (usually arm movement to leg movements), increasing range of motion, and using repetition. According to my participants, incorporating the use of several body parts to increase complexity of movement was often considered a progression. Michelle and Lee stated that the class usually began with an exercise for the legs and then slowly, other parts, such as arm movements, were added. Modifications of different exercises progressed the students towards mastering the final skill. Michelle, Lee, Addison, and Amy all agreed that the instructor needed to provide one or two modifications. They all talked about three specific modifications in their class that were important: (1) arm movement options: on the waist or in a specific ballet arm position; (2) the height of leg lifts: option of having the leg on the floor or at forty-five degrees or even higher; (3) option of third or fifth position of feet.

In summary, the ballet movements challenge the beginner ballet dancers because they require detailed technical execution as well as a certain precise quality. The instructor plays a critical role by facilitating the learning process through progression of modifications and feedback of the performance. Similar to my participants, Hamera (2005) describes ballet as the bodies' and communities' relationships to space, time, and the movements created in their intersections. Following Foucault (1995), the organization of ballet movements into series of exercises and then larger combinations based on regulated time, the bodily movement, and space functions as a disciplinary technique. Docility, then, is a result of such exercises, precise control of the operations, and positions of the body through repetition. The ballet movements described by my participants seemed to embody many of these qualities. Consequently, while learning the traditional movements of ballet can be beneficial, it can also create docile dancers.

Conclusion

In this study, my purpose was to examine beginner ballet dancers' and their instructor's views of their class. Space, time, and move-ment all encompassed aspects of discipline in a beginner ballet class. Based on my interviews, the ballet space was an important aspect of participants' experiences through the structure of the class, visibility, and observation. The continual observation was often a result of the permanent visibility afforded by the functional ballet space where exercises were performed at the barre, the cen-tre, and moving across the floor. The class was structured efficiently to emphasize proper timing of a number of repeated exercises with music. While some participants questioned the need for such preci-sion, they all accepted the time as an aspect of a proper ballet class. Finally, ballet required precise articulation of different body parts in graceful movements. While this was a challenge in the beginner class, the instructor played a critical role in facilitating the process of learning the exacting ballet movements. The instructor guided, observed, and provided feedback for the beginner dancers. Similar to the use of space and time, the dancers in my study were aware of the preconceived ideas of the movements that needed to be learned in a beginner ballet class. The instructor also followed the traditions of ballet technique training but was open to experimenting with new ways of teaching.

At the same time, many of the dancers enjoyed learning ballet technique in their class and aspired to improve their ability to dance. In this sense, disciplinary practices were also a source of pleasure. My findings are, in many ways, similar to Dryburgh and Fortin (2010), who acknowledge that space, time, and movement interact to create complex yet fluid relationships for professional ballet dancers. Kolb and Kalogeropoulou (2012) add that scholars often criticize ballet and never look at the real notion of pleasure of participating in a ballet class. Atencio and Wright (2009) also conclude that young people often take up embodied practices of ballet as a form of expression that allows them to feel valued.

Based on my results, I now acknowledge that many dancers enjoy the structured traditional ballet class, which is designed to efficiently improve the dancers' technique. However, as a ballet instructor, I also need to be mindful of how I deliver my material to the dancers to create thinking dancers instead of docile bodies. I further recognize that it is important to avoid a strict disciplinary practice (Foucault, 1995) when learning and teaching ballet. I conclude that the ballet technique training does not need to produce entirely disciplined dancers, or does not need to be entirely "bad." Based on my findings, however, disciplinary techniques of space, time, and movement in traditional ballet training were often unquestioningly accepted, but my participants also seemed willing to explore less disciplinary ways to learn ballet.

As Green (2003) reaffirms, "It is important to change the way we teach dance in order to change what is valued in dance" (98). Thus, I conclude my study by stressing the importance of ballet instructors to reinforce ethical ballet practices when teaching a beginner ballet class. It is necessary to create more meaningful practices for the beginner ballet dancer because they will ultimately lessen the docility more than practices adopted directly from dancers in professional training. Following Markula and Pringle (2006), who explain that "Foucault's ideas on how to make the social world a more harmonious place focused on the ability of people to cultivate a new sense of self and more ethical modes of existence" (38), my hope is to engage more ethically as an instructor, as well as to create thinking dancers instead of docile bodies. As Ritenburg (2010) states, "not only will these [new teaching practices] open new possibilities for broader and healthier participation in ballet but [they will] also contribute to encouraging aesthetic innovation and development in ballet" (82). Based on my study, I look towards developing an effective, accessible, and, above all, ethical ballet class.

References

Aalten, A. (1995). In the presence of the body: Theorizing training, injuries and pain in ballet. *Dance Research Journal, 37*(2), 55–72.

Adame, D., Blumenkehl, N., Cole, S., & Radell, S. (2011). The impact of mirrors on body image and performance in high and low performing female ballet students. *Journal of Dance Medicine & Science, 15*(3), 108–16.

Anshel, M. H. (2004). Sources of disordered eating patterns between ballet dancers and non-dancers. *Journal of Sport Behavior, 27*(2), 115–33.

Atencio, G., & Wright, J. (2009). "Ballet it's too whitey": Discursive hierarchies of high school dance spaces and the constitution of embodied feminine subjectivities. *Gender & Education, 21,* 31–46.

Barr, S., & Risner, D. (2014). Weaving social foundations through dance pedagogy: A pedagogy of uncovering. *Journal of Dance Education, 14,* 136–45.

Benn, T., & Walters, D. (2001). Between Scylla and Charybdis: Nutritional education versus body culture and the ballet aesthetic: The effects on the lives of female dancers. *Research in Dance Education, 2,* 139–54.

Bettle, N., Bettle, O., Neumarker, U., & Neumarker, K. J. (2001). Body image and self-esteem in adolescent ballet dancers. *Perceptual and Motor Skills, 93*(1), 297–309.

Dryburgh, A., & Fortin, S. (2010). Weighing in on surveillance: Perception of the impact of surveillance on female ballet dancers' health. *Research in Dance Education, 11,* 95–108.

Foucault, M. (1995). *Discipline and punish: The birth of the prison.* (A. Sheridan, Trans.). New York: Vintage.

Fraleigh, S., & Hanstein, P. (1999). *Researching dance: Evolving modes of inquiry.* Pittsburgh, PA: University Pittsburgh Press.

Franko, M. (2011). Archaeological choreographic practices: Foucault and Forsythe. *History of the Human Sciences, 24*(4), 97–112.

Garrich, J. G., & Reque, R. K. (1993). Ballet injuries: An analysis of epidemiology and financial outcome. *The American Journal of Sports Medicine, 21,* 586–90.

Green, J. (1999). Somatic authority and the myth of the ideal body in dance education. *Dance Research Journal, 31*(2), 80–100.

Green, J. (2003). Foucault and the training of docile bodies in dance education. *The Journal of the Arts and Learning Special Interest Group of the American Education Research Association, 19,* 99–125.

Hamera, J. (2005). All the (dis)comforts of home: Place, gendered self-fashioning, and solidarity in a ballet studio. *Text & Performance Quarterly, 25*(2), 93–112.

Kolb, A., & Kalogeropoulou, S. (2012). In defence of ballet: Women, agency and the philosophy of pleasure. *Dance Research: The Journal of the Society for Dance Research, 30*(2), 107–25.

Markula, P., & Pringle, R. (2006). *Foucault, sport and exercise: Power, knowledge and transforming the self.* New York: Routledge.

Markula, P., & Silk, M. (2011). *Qualitative research for physical culture.* Basingstoke, UK: Palgrave.

McEwen, K., & Young, K. (2011). Ballet and pain: Reflections on a risk-dance culture. *Qualitative Research in Sport, Exercise & Health, 3*(2), 152–73.

Ritenburg, H. (2010). Frozen landscapes: A Foucauldian genealogy of the ideal ballet dancer's body. *Research in Dance Education, 11,* 71–85.

Ravaldi, C., Vannacci, A., Bolognesi, E., Mancini, S., Faravelli, C., & Ricca, V. (2006). Gender role, eating disorder symptoms, and body image concern in ballet dancers. *Journal of Psychosomatic Research, 61,* 529–35.

Shapiro, S. B. (1998). Toward transformative teachers: Critical and feminist perspectives in dance education. In S. B. Shapiro (Ed.), *Dance, power, and difference: Critical and feminist perspectives on dance education* (7–21). Champaign, IL: Human Kinetics.

Tiggemann, M., & Slater, A. (2001). A test of objectification theory in former dancers and non-dancers. *Psychology of Women Quarterly, 25*(1), 57–64.

Turner, B. S., & Wainwright, S. P. (2003). Corps de ballet: The case of the injured ballet dancer. *Sociology of Health & Illness, 25,* 269–88.

Wainwright, S. P., & Turner, B. S. (2004). Epiphanies of embodiment: Injury, identity and the balletic body. *Qualitative Research, 4,* 311–37.

Whittier, C. (2006). Laban movement analysis approach to classical ballet pedagogy. *Journal of Dance Education, 6,* 124–32.

7

BALLET FOR ALL BODIES?

Tensions in Teaching Ballet Technique within
an Integrated Dance Context

Kelsie Acton and Lindsay Eales

Integrated dance brings together people who experience disability
and those who do not to dance, create, and perform in an effort
to make the highly exclusionary practice of dance more inclusive
(Benjamin, 2002). Albright (1997) points to ballet's investment in
a specific body type, in particular the image of the sylph, which
exemplifies "an aesthetic of beauty, grace, and line" (306), and
suggests that integrated dance holds possibilities for questioning
ballet's ableist notions of an ideal dancer's body. Integrated dance,
as improvisational and community-driven, differs significantly
from technically precise and elitist ballet. Despite these differences, we propose an integrated, *inclusive* ballet technique in this
chapter. Inclusive technique is a way of teaching ballet (along
with other dance techniques such as jazz or contemporary) in an
integrated context that works to undo assumptions about how
bodies *should* move, while providing dancers with tools and choices
about how they train their bodies. We use the tools of Foucauldian
theory, components of Laban movement analysis, brain-compatible
dance education, traditional ballet technique, and the practices of

adaptation and transformation to construct our inclusive ballet pedagogy. To unpack this inclusive ballet pedagogy, we first discuss the context for integrated dance at both professional and community levels as well as our own involvement in integrated dance. We then review previous literature on integrated dance before discussing our theoretical lenses. Using Foucauldian concepts of discipline and normalization (Foucault, 1995), we examine the pleasures and dangers inherent in the discipline involved in ballet training. We then use a conversational format to illustrate how we blend the practices of brain-compatible dance (Gilbert, 2006), Laban's "efforts" (Laban, 1971), as well as movement adaptation and transformation to provide our dancers the tools to create ballet technique for themselves. We also discuss some of the productive tensions that arise from combining these frameworks within our pedagogical practice.

Contextualizing Our Integrated Dance Practices

There are several professional integrated dance companies worldwide, mostly in North America and Europe. Their performances exhibit a variety of movement vocabularies, but professional integrated companies such as Candoco, based in London, AXIS Dance of California, and Dancing Wheels of Cleveland draw upon ballet and contemporary dance. In Canada, however, Propeller Dance of Ottawa and Momo Dance Theatre of Calgary primarily use improvisational techniques. Training at a community level, nevertheless, is typically based on creative movement and contact improvisation (Benjamin, 2002; Kaufmann, 2006; DanceAbility International, n.d.).

Working in integrated dance in Edmonton, Alberta, we noticed this discontinuity between community and professional integrated dance. Edmonton is home to Solidance Inclusive Recreation Society, which runs the city's only community-based integrated dance classes (Solidance, 2015). In addition, Edmonton is home to

CRIPSiE (Collaborative Radically Integrated Performers Society in Edmonton), a professional disability art collective with a focus on integrated dance. We both work with CRIPSiE and Solidance, and are PHD students at the University of Alberta studying disability and dance. However, for this article we will focus on the recreational class we run through Solidance. Lindsay is a certified occupational therapist and has trained with some of the world leaders in integrated dance. Kelsie is an experienced dance instructor and certified yoga teacher. Solidance has grown from a small weekly class, running from March to July, to an incorporated, not-for-profit organization delivering inclusive recreational movement programming year round. The programming is focused on removing barriers—financial, social, and physical—to participation in movement-based recreation. The community is diverse; our participants are of all ages and abilities, and what unites them is a love of inclusive movement.

While Solidance is recreational, over the years, some of our dancers have sought out professional performance opportunities with CRIPSiE. To transition to a more professional integrated dance setting, they need movement tools such as the ability to adapt set movement phrases to their body, to recall choreography (to varying degrees), and to navigate rhythm and timing of unison choreography (see Irving & Giles, 2011). That said, dancers who have no plans to engage with professional integrated dance have expressed desire to learn movement skills that are offered through traditional dance techniques. This desire surfaced in A New Constellation, a "danceumentary" following members of our dance community as they rehearsed for a performance. In the documentary, a dancer, Iris, states, "5, 6, 7, 8 and I thought, I'm home, I'm home" (DuVal, Eales, Peers, & Ulanicki, 2013). For Iris, who had danced as an adult before beginning to use a wheelchair later in life, using a precise count was an essential, familiar, and deeply desirable part of dance class. She desired a precise count, typical of ballet training, to accompany her movement in order to feel that she was dancing again. This desire for the embodied pleasures of technical dance training keeps us attached to deriving methods for integrated dance instruction that are inclusive yet based on traditional dance vocabularies. One way we do this is to draw upon published literature, both academic and practical, that offers methods and best practices for teaching integrated dance.

Pedagogy in Integrated Dance

There is a growing body of literature on integrated dance pedagogy (Cheesman, 2011; Herman & Chatfield, 2010; Østern, 2009; Stran & Hardin, 2002; Whatley, 2007; Zitomer, 2013) and the transition from recreational to professional integrated dance (Irving & Giles, 2011; Aujla & Redding, 2013, 2014). Scholars have explored integrated dance pedagogical practices through questionnaires (Herman & Chatfield, 2010; Whatley, 2007), interviews with integrated dancers (Irving & Giles, 2011; Østern, 2009; Whatley, 2007), class observation (Irving & Giles, 2011; Whatley, 2007), and interviews with instructors (Irving & Giles, 2011; Zitomer, 2013). Several studies detail barriers experienced by dancers seeking integrated dance training. These include attitudinal barriers, wherein dancers with disabilities as well as their parents, friends, and teachers do not think they are capable of participating in dance (Aujla & Redding, 2013; Zitomer & Reid, 2011); logistical barriers such as lack of transportation and physical access to dance spaces (Aujla & Redding, 2013); and aesthetic barriers that dancers face when educators and audiences typically value normative bodies and movement qualities that are inaccessible to many body types (Aujla & Redding, 2013; Whatley, 2007). Both Aujla and Redding (2013) and Whatley (2007) note that dancers who experience disability face another barrier: a lack of traditional dance "technique" training.

In an effort to address both attitudinal and aesthetic barriers to dance training, integrated dance scholars and practitioners have largely focused on improvisation and contact improvisation as the main pedagogical practice within integrated dance, as opposed to traditional technique training (Herman & Chatfield, 2010; Østern, 2009; Irving & Giles, 2011). These authors suggest that contact improvisation provides more accessible entry points into dance practice than traditional technique such as ballet.

Integrated dance training manuals also offer insight into the most common pedagogical approaches to integrated dance. Much like the focus of scholarly articles on integrated dance, most of this work is grounded in creative movement and improvisation. For example, Benjamin (2002) leads the reader through a series of improvisation exercises to create inclusive dance classes. Benjamin contextualizes this approach by providing stories of the founding of Candoco, the first professional integrated dance company, and integrated community dance projects he has led since. This manual has provided much guidance to our pedagogical practice in running recreational integrated dance classes, specifically increasing our focus on improvisation. Kaufmann's (2006) text focuses on teaching children, but, likewise, offers us a series of creative movement exercises and games that encourage people to explore various possible ways of moving. Finally, DanceAbility, the only company offering a teacher's certification in integrated dance, foregrounds contact improvisation as the basis for its training (DanceAbility International, n.d.). In an interview with Jenna Malarkey, Alito Alessi (2003), DanceAbility founder, establishes improvisation as central to his pedagogy, movement, and political agenda, stating, "besides encouraging freedom from habit, improvisation also expands our potential for expressing ourselves" (Malarkey & Alessi, 2003). Davies (2008) aligns with Alessi's philosophy, crediting contact improvisation as the dance form responsible for "widening the range and definition of acceptable dance bodies" (44). This sentiment is echoed in the wider literature on contact improvisation, notably by Novack (1990), who positions contact improvisation as an egalitarian alternative to ballet. She states, "Ballet requires exaggerated sexual dimorphism because the man must be able to lift the woman with ease" (128). In contrast, "in a contact improvisation duet...any kind of...body is acceptable because the form depends on sensing moment and changing from active to passive weight at the right moments" (128). Thus, according to Novack (1990), the skills and bodies demanded by ballet are very different from those demanded by contact improvisation.

With the focus so predominantly on contact improvisation in most literature on integrated dance pedagogy, how do we reconcile the demands of traditional technical dance training in forms such as ballet with the expressive and inclusive potentials of improvisation and creative movement? A few scholars have provided some insights into how to structure classes to best facilitate the skill development of integrated dancers (Aujla & Redding, 2014; Whatley, 2007; Zitomer, 2013). For example, Zitomer (2013) offers us some guidance in her phenomenological exploration of integrated dance pedagogy. The author argues that creating successful integrated dance programming is done through consistent class routines, respecting student choices, and a willingness on behalf of the instructor to make mistakes and learn from them in front of the class.

Aujla and Redding (2014) also provide guidance for structuring meaningful pedagogy for integrated dancers. These authors conducted interviews with integrated dance teachers and choreographers to determine the pedagogical needs of integrated dancers in their transition from recreational to professional dance. These needs include extending the amount of time available for training, fostering adaptation skills, utilizing repetition, setting high physical standards, and offering tools for improving physical fitness of dancers in the process of professionalizing. While some of these needs may be less relevant in recreational settings (such as cross-training for fitness or demanding high standards), it is still relevant to consider translating some of these needs into the recreational context. For example, training adaptation skills and repetition allow dancers to access a variety of dance and movement environments beyond the integrated dance class.

Whatley (2007) also offers some important insights by specifically focusing on the training of "technique" as opposed to contact improvisation. The author used group interviews, questionnaires, and class feedback to explore the perspectives of both disabled and non-disabled students in a UK–based post-secondary dance program. When teaching technique to disabled and non-disabled dancers, dancers experiencing disabilities articulated that they felt their "deficiencies" were more apparent and that they compared themselves heavily to non-disabled dancers. Further, they found focusing on sensation to be discouraging, as their embodiment and sensation did not align with normative bodily instruction. They did, however, appreciate smaller class size where they did not feel like the minority. To overcome the negative experiences, Whatley (2007) suggests focusing on communicating clear goals for each movement activity; providing demonstration that lead to examples of how to translate and adapt movement; offering a clear articulation of the anatomical purpose of the exercise as well as alternative ways of sensing the body; and facilitating repetition and variation of exercises.

We argue that the guidelines for successful programming offered by Zitomer (2013), Aujla and Redding (2014), and Whatley (2007) can be implemented in any integrated dance class, regardless of what specific form of dance is being taught. We want to hold onto the pleasures of teaching ballet within an integrated context, while maintaining the positive potentials of creative movement and improvisation to expand which bodies can access dance. To do so, we must ask, what is potentially problematic about teaching ballet in an integrated dance environment? Also, learning from these scholars, what do we need to shift in the practice of ballet training to facilitate skill development while respecting student choices, offering freedom of expression, and increasing accessibility through adaptation and improvisation?

Foucault in the Ballet Class

Analyzing ballet pedagogy from a Foucauldian perspective offers us the opportunity to critique taken-for-granted practices in ballet pedagogy, such as the use of mirrors, ranking, time-tabling, and the connection between movement and music (Clark, 2014). As Clark (2014) demonstrates, recreational ballet classes are disciplinary spaces where space, time, and movement are controlled for increased surveillance to make adolescent girls skilled dancers, but docile bodies. Dryburgh and Fortin (2010) found that professional ballet dancers viewed surveillance, particularly the surveillance of body weight, as both positive and negative in their efforts to discipline their bodies towards the ballet ideal. Likewise, Green (2001) demonstrates that post-secondary dance students are subjected to surveillance and self-surveillance. Green (2001) also examines how dancers used somatics (practices involving embodied felt connections to movement as opposed to viewing the body as an object) to resist the disciplinary and normalizing space of their technique classes. According to these researchers, discipline is a predominant feature of the practice of ballet.

Irving and Giles (2011), in their Foucauldian study of a Canadian integrated dance company's transition from a recreational group into an increasingly professional company, support these findings. These authors conducted an ethnographic study and interviews with members of the company, and then used Foucauldian discourse analysis, to explore how these dancers navigated, resisted, and created alternatives to dominant discourses of professional dance. As part of their exploration, they also examined the company's rehearsal practices. The authors note that "the organization and dancers find themselves wanting to advance their technique, grow the group's artistry and gain recognition as valid and professional artists" (383), while at the same time working to challenge dominant discourses and practices regarding how dancers should look and move. The dancers discussed encountering disciplinary techniques such as timing, spacing, and repetition largely in relation to learning choreography. They conclude that implementing disciplinary techniques around timing, spacing, memorization, and repetition were points of struggle where integrated dancers resisted, rejected, and/or failed to be "successful" (despite the desire to be disciplined). The dancers shared the concern that focusing heavily on these disciplinary practices would decrease the accessibility of their dance form, but also shared a continuing desire to develop new skills, individually and as a group, through this type of training. This particular research project resonated with our own experiences within integrated dance settings, where there are ongoing tensions between dancers' desires for discipline imposed by technical training and the overarching critiques of the inaccessible and exclusionary practices of traditional dance forms such as ballet.

Despite critiques of the disciplinary nature of dance, particularly ballet, from both ballet scholars and integrated dance scholars, ballet is a popular recreational activity for many girls and women (Kolb & Kalogeropoulou, 2012). Kolb and Kalogeropoulou's (2012) research with recreational adult ballet dancers reveals that it is the disciplinary elements and the pursuit of perfection that draw women to ballet training. The women they interviewed explicitly cited the discipline, the clear guidelines for achievement and progression, and the relinquishing of control as motivation for pursuing ballet as a recreational activity. Likewise, Hamera (2007) found in her ethnography of an elite ballet studio that the adolescent girls there engaged with ballet, and specifically the discipline required by ballet, as a form of embodied resistance against the pressures and demands of contemporary society. Further, Clark (2014) notes that for her adolescent dancers, "it was the structure of dance movement (which was enabled through disciplinary power) that pointed to these positive creative experiences" of "skillful bodily movement and the subsequent exhilarating physical[ity]" (212). Regardless of the potential dangers of discipline, some dancers in our community, ourselves included, like Kolb and Kalogeropoulou's (2012) adult ballet dancers and Clark's (2014) young ballet dancers, find pleasure and enjoyment in some of the disciplinary aspects of ballet. Following McWhorter (1999), we ask,

"what if we deliberately...engaged in graduated disciplinary practices for their own sake—for the pleasures they bring—rather than
for some goal beyond them?" (182).

In response to our own, often pleasurable, experiences of ballet
training, and the desire from our community for this type of training, Lindsay began to develop a way of teaching ballet (and other
forms of dance technique) that would give dancers the ability to
choose a suitable ballet technique for themselves. In the following
section, we engage in a dialogue to outline our class structure and
some pedagogical choices we make to facilitate inclusive ballet
technique. This inclusive technique aims to offer the pleasures of
some of the disciplinary aspects of ballet while making space for
choice and adaptation in our class. Increasingly, there have been
calls for qualitative researchers to engage in multi-voiced, reflexive, and dialogic texts (Denzin & Lincoln, 2011) to represent their
research findings. We chose to represent our research as an "essay-
istic personal experience" dialogue (Markula & Silk, 2011, 183).
This form of writing invites the reader "to share or learn, from a
researcher's personal experiences, about the social construction of
a self in a specific context" (Markula & Silk, 2011, 183). In this case,
we invite the reader to learn from our personal experiences about
the construction of a pedagogical practice in the context of integrated dance. Since our pedagogical practice has evolved through
conversations, we feel a dialogue best represents the ongoing
process of collaborative reflection that we engage in to interrogate
our own practice. Through this conversation we also discuss some
of the productive tensions and ongoing debates we have around
instructing inclusive ballet technique.

Building Our Inclusive Ballet Environment

KELSIE: Our class sessions are usually run weekly for three or four
months. Should we repeat a warm-up from week to week?

LINDSAY: Foucault (1995) identifies repetition as one of the ways bodies are disciplined and normalized. However, I remember Zitomer (2013) suggesting that dancers might feel more secure with a section of the class that is consistent from week to week.

KELSIE: What if we began with creative movement, so the parameters of the improvisation are the same, but dancers can move differently?

LINDSAY: Perfect. In fact, let's begin each session with several classes of creative movement to foreground the movement skills that dancers already have in their vocabulary, and to develop comfort in the space and with each other. We can then move on to teach more traditional forms of dance technique including ballet, jazz, and contemporary.

KELSIE: We can create comfort by loosely structuring each of the classes through brain-compatible dance education lesson planning (Gilbert, 2006). Brain-compatible dance combines developmental movement patterns and choreographic concepts into instructional strategies for teaching dance to people of all ages and abilities. This structure relies heavily on Laban's efforts. The efforts are part of Laban's attempt to create a system to describe and facilitate movement. Although modern and contemporary dance classes are more likely to use the efforts than a ballet class, I think they'll be useful to us. Each week we'll take a movement concept such as weight, space, body parts, or relationships, and structure the class and how we teach any set movement through a concept. In addition, brain-compatible dance education encourages a balance between instructor-led and learner-led exercises, with the inclusion of warm-up, concept exploration, skill development, choreographic exploration, and cool-down. We can also start every class with BrainDance! BrainDance, remember, is composed of eight developmental movement patterns that humans generally move through in the first year of life (Gilbert, 2006). Perhaps everyone can start with this?

Warm-up: Rejecting Therapeutic Normalization in the Inclusive Ballet Setting

LINDSAY: How do we avoid the therapeutic language around BrainDance? It is generally articulated as a movement tool to improve neurological functioning at any stage of life (Gilbert, 2006).

KELSIE: What's wrong with therapeutic movement?

LINDSAY: Well...The process and forces of medicalization pervade the lives of people experiencing disability. Every activity of a person experiencing disability comes to be understood through the lens of therapy, which assumes that their bodies and minds are not right and must perpetually be improved (Withers, 2012). Most forms of therapy assume that there is an ideal human body whose systems and limbs function in a particular relation to each other, an ideal mind that functions in a particular way, and that people should perpetually strive to create these ideal states of functioning. Many types of violence have been perpetrated against people experiencing disability in the name of medical treatment, including sterilization, forced or experimental surgery, institutionalization, and exhibition (Albrecht, 1992; Withers, 2012). When medicalization has so many consequences for people experiencing disability, it seems an ethical imperative to create a dance class where people are subjected to as little medicalization as possible.

KELSIE: Wow. Okay, I agree we shouldn't use medical or therapeutic language in our class. What if we still utilize the BrainDance movements, since it offers a lot of variety and structure in improvisation? I want dancers to get an extensive body warm-up with the freedom to choose how they engage with each movement. It also challenges dancers to explore movement they may not ordinarily engage with such as moving one side of the body and cross lateral movement. What if we use the movement but never discuss its therapeutic roots?

LINDSAY: That seems like a fair compromise. But I want some set elements to the warm-up because some of our dancers have asked for a set warm-up. They say that they want a set series of movements through which they can judge where their body is at each week and experience any bodily progression they may have over the weeks.

KELSIE: That's fascinating. Foucault (1995) would suggest that it might reflect a self-imposed desire for progression towards an ideal that does not exist? But as a dancer I completely understand that desire!

LINDSAY: So, the rest of the movement in the warm-up will be reminiscent of a traditional jazz/contemporary dance class warm-up, but our cueing should build in options into the sequence such as "Move to the floor if that is comfortable for you."

KELSIE: Importantly, we've developed this set series of warm-up movements with members of the dance community who have diverse embodiments, so the warm-up is relevant to the movements they want to explore and taught in a way that has multiple entry points for adapting movement as desired.

The Barre: Discipline and Pleasure in Inclusive Ballet Technique

LINDSAY: Following our set warm-up, during our exploration of ballet technique we'll typically begin with exercises at the "barre," which is often the wall because our dance space is in a gymnasium and not a ballet studio.

KELSIE: You taught inclusive dance for a number of years before I joined the class. Did you always teach ballet barre?

LINDSAY: From the first session of integrated dance classes I taught, I have always included an exploration of ballet as well as jazz and contemporary dance technique. To be honest, initially this was only because I did not know how to teach integrated dance, and I had no familiarity with contact improvisation as the foundation of much of integrated dance pedagogy worldwide. All I had for pedagogical tools were my experiences in traditional dance settings, learning traditional dance techniques such as ballet, and my burgeoning skills in adaptation from my occupational therapy education.

KELSIE: Were you as reflective about your pedagogy when you started as you are now?

LINDSAY: At first, I had little critical thought about how teaching traditional dance technique might be dangerous, and I just fell back on what I had been taught. I also had no exposure to Foucault's (1995) theoretical concept of disciplinary techniques, the implications and dangers of these techniques, and the ways that these techniques are enacted within the ballet environment.

KELSIE: Honestly, I think we're still holding on to a lot of disciplinary elements of traditional ballet. When we teach ballet technique by introducing a single movement, such as a tendu at the barre, we're still holding on to the typical progression of a ballet class by introducing barre work early on. Much of our class reproduces the disciplinary nature of elite ballet classes. Although we practice without mirrors, we maintain a number of disciplinary aspects regarding space, time, and surveillance. For example, dancers come to class in a specific place designed for movement and stagger themselves to avoid collisions and maintain optimal lines of sight. Class is held at a specific time and follows a timetable that we have carefully established. And we ask dancers to co-ordinate their movements to the rhythm of the music. Foucault's (1995) notion of "the organization of genesis," specifically the act of organizing events to occur in a progressive manner, is relevant to this practice of progressively structuring our inclusive ballet classes.

LINDSAY: Foucault (1995) notes that progression becomes a way of ranking people according to ability and approximation towards an ideal body. What if we're reinforcing the hyper-able ballet body through our use of progressions?

KELSIE: Maybe we are. But McWhorter (1999) suggests that "instead of rejecting disciplinary practices altogether—which we could not in any case do—what we need are disciplinary practices that we might engage in carefully, deliberately, but with modifications that mitigate against standardized outcomes" (181). We need to work to be careful and deliberate in our implementation of disciplinary techniques. We must always try to offer choice and space for modification, and try to validate all choices and modifications as being of equal value. We need to attempt to get rid of the notion of an ideal.

LINDSAY: For example, dancers are given the choice to explore the barre exercise from the centre of the room if they want to. For some people, this choice to move in the centre of the room may be about challenging their sense of balance, while for others it might be about finding a better sight line to the instructor. This is one way our use of space is more flexible than in a traditional ballet class.

Centre Work: Adaptation and Transformation

LINDSAY: In relation to offering opportunities for modifications to our instruction, one important distinction we have come to make in teaching our ballet classes, and which has informed all of our pedagogy beyond ballet, is the difference between movement adaptation and movement transformation. Generally speaking, most beginning ballet movements work the legs, which is not accessible to a number of our dancers. To introduce more inclusive movement options, we often need to demonstrate how the movement might be *adapted*.

KELSIE: For example, dancers may engage with the exercise by using the arms instead of the legs.

LINDSAY: In my practical experience, the technique of adaptation is a very common strategy in integrated dance.

KELSIE: Shifting the movement to the arms, however, does not guarantee that there will be accessible options for all our dancers, as our dancers utilize a variety of mobility tools, have diverse embodiments, and diverse access to movement of their limbs. To increase the accessibility of this movement exercise further, what if we seek to *transform* the movement? We do this by asking the class what the meaning, intention, or quality of the movement is, and encouraging dancers to embody that quality in any part of their body they wish to. For example, the meaning of *tendu* in English is "to stretch or draw tight." Taking this meaning literally, we can ask our dancers how many ways they can stretch or draw tight different parts of their bodies, or the relations of their bodies to each other and the larger space around them.

LINDSAY: Another example is *plié*, which means "to bend or fold." We would, thus, ask our dancers how they can fold or bend any part of their body. Or how they can bend in relation to each other. This focus on the meaning or intention of the movement drastically expands the ways dancers can relate to and transform traditional ballet vocabulary.

KELSIE: Laban's "efforts" provide a vocabulary to describe movement in order for dancers to transform the meaning or intention of traditional ballet vocabulary in increasingly expanded ways, based on movement quality. Laban's (1971) efforts consist of weight, space, time, and flow. Each of these efforts is understood on a binary scale.

LINDSAY: For example, the "weight" effort can consist of a "strong resistance of weight and of a movement sensation, heavy" (Laban, 1971, 76) or a "weak resistance to weight and of a movement sensation, light or a feel of weightlessness" (76). The "flow" effort is described along the axis of bound and unbound movement, where movement demonstrates either "a liberating or withholding attitude towards flow" (76).

KELSIE: By adjusting the relationship to each *effort*, dancers can produce different movement qualities and, within the framework of technical ballet training, different movements. Our example, a tendu, or an extension of the foot along the floor, can be described as a moderately heavy (weight), direct (space), moderately slow (time), and moderately bound (flow) movement. The idea "to stretch or draw tight" and the particular *efforts* that inform tendu are the movement qualities that our dancers play with when they adapt and transform the movement.

LINDSAY: While the movement vocabulary provided by Laban's movement analysis framework is extremely useful in integrated dance contexts, I have some reservations about the foundational assumptions that are put forth. According to Moore and Yamamoto (2012), Laban asserted that movement is natural, authentic, intentional, patterned, and orderly. This articulation posits an essentialist and normative way of moving, something that can and should be called into question by a poststructuralist theoretical perspective. Foucault (1995) taught us that bodies are not natural and orderly, but that disciplinary techniques produce bodies that come to be understood as natural, essential, patterned, and orderly.

KELSIE: I would argue a little with that. Laban (1988) often described movement as unintentional, arising as a product of the interactions between the moving body and its environment. However, I think it's safe to say that Laban did have a therapeutic bent and saw movement as ideally controlled, intentional, and encompassing a wide variety of possible ways of moving (Laban, 1988), a range that may not be accessible to all bodies.

Conclusion: A Reverence to Valuing Ballet in Integrated Dance

A reverence is a movement practice used to close out a ballet class, and is intended to honour and celebrate the work that has been done within the class. Borrowing from this ballet tradition, we would like to offer a reverence here: a reverence that celebrates the critical work being done in many integrated dance contexts to make dance more accessible, and that also honours the value of teaching inclusive ballet technique within these contexts. Instead of demanding the strict control of movement that assumes a normative and idealized body, we hope to open the range of possible movements and provide our dancers with tools to make choices about how they will move in relationship to traditional ballet vocabulary. We, nevertheless, believe strongly in the importance of learning traditional ballet vocabulary. First, this type of technique allows our dancers to access socially valued and understood dance vocabularies. A number of our participants have family members or friends who have trained in ballet. To engage with ballet gives them a shared experience with family and peers that training in improvisational techniques may not. This argument is echoed by Goodwin, Krohn, and Kuhnle (2004), who found that children in a segregated dance program gained common experiences of dance training that enabled relational connections with their peers.

Second, exposing integrated dancers to traditional dance vocabulary and providing them tools to explore these vocabularies with their own bodies provides the opportunity for dancers to seek training in other (more traditional) classes beyond our recreational programming. Several of our dancers, while still training with us, have gone on to access training in the broader recreational dance community. We would argue that in moving beyond our recreational dance classes, dancers experiencing disability who take classes in other environments challenge other dance instructors to consider the inclusivity of their own pedagogical practices.

Finally, the pleasures of dance training, particularly ballet training, are not ones that should be denied to our dancers because of physical, social, or financial barriers. We hope this conversation offers insight into how we teach inclusive ballet technique and, most importantly, how we reflect on and question our pedagogical choices.

References

Albrecht, G. L. (1992). *The disability business: Rehabilitation in America*. Newbury Park, CA: Sage Publications.

Albright, A.C. (1997). *Choreographing difference: The body and identity in contemporary dance*. Middletown, CT: Wesleyan University Press.

Aujla, I. J., & Redding, E. (2013). Barriers to dance training for young people with disabilities. *British Journal of Special Education, 40*(2), 80–85. doi:10.1111/1467-8578.12021

Aujla, I. J., & Redding, E. (2014). The identification and development of talented young dancers with disabilities. *Research in Dance Education, 15*, 54–70. doi:10.1080/14647893.2012.721762

Benjamin, A. (2002). *Making an entrance: Theory and practice for disabled and non-disabled dancers*. London: Routledge.

Cheesman, S. (2011). Facilitating dance making from a teacher's perspective within a community integrated dance class. *Research in Dance Education, 12*, 29–40. doi:10.1080/14647893.2011.554976

Clark, M. (2014). *Dancing the self: How girls who dance in commercial dance studios construct a self through the dancing body* (Unpublished doctoral dissertation). University of Alberta, Edmonton.

DanceAbility International (n.d.). DanceAbility teacher certification. Retrieved from http://www.danceability.com/teacher.php

Davies, T. (2008). Mobility: AXIS dancers push the boundaries of access. *Text & Performance Quarterly, 28*(1/2), 43–63. doi:10.1080/10462930701754309

Denzin, N. K., & Lincoln, Y. S. (2011). Introduction: The discipline and practice of qualitative research. In N. K. Denzin & Y. S. Lincoln (Eds.), *The SAGE handbook of qualitative research* (1–20). Thousand Oaks, CA: Sage.

Dryburgh, A., & Fortin, S. (2010). Weighing in on surveillance: Perception of the impact of surveillance on female ballet dancers' health. *Research in Dance Education, 11*, 95–108.

DuVal, J., Eales, L., Peers, D., & Ulanicki, R. (Producers & Directors). (2013). *The new constellation: A dance-umentary* [Motion picture]. Canada.

Foucault, M. (1995). *Discipline and punish: The birth of the prison.* (A. Sheridan, Trans.). Toronto: Random House.

Goodwin, D. L., Krohn, J., & Kuhnle, A. (2004). Beyond the wheelchair: The experience of dance. *Adapted Physical Activity Quarterly, 21*, 229–47.

Green, J. (2001). Socially constructed bodies in American dance classrooms. *Research in Dance Education, 2*, 155–73.

Gilbert, A. G. (2006). *Brain-compatible dance education*. Reston, VA: National Dance Association.

Hamera, J. (2007). *Dancing communities: Performance, difference, and connection in the global city*. Basingstoke, UK: Palgrave Macmillian.

Herman, A., & Chatfield, S. (2010). A detailed analysis of DanceAbility's contribution to mixed-ability dance. *Journal of Dance Education, 10*, 41–55.

Irving, H. R., & Giles, A. R. (2011). A dance revolution? Responding to dominant discourses in contemporary integrated dance. *Leisure/Loisir: Journal of the Canadian Association for Leisure Studies, 35*, 371–89. doi:10.1080/14927713.2011.648415

Kaufmann, K. A. (2006). *Inclusive creative movement and dance*. Champaign, IL: Human Kinetics.

Kolb, A., & Kalogeropoulou, S. (2012). In defence of ballet: Women, agency and the philosophy of pleasure. *Dance Research, 30*(2), 107–25. doi:10.3366/drs.2012.0042

Laban, R. (1971). *The mastery of movement*. London: MacDonald & Evans.

Laban, R. (1988). *Modern educational dance*. Plymouth, UK: Norcote Publishing.

Malarkey, J., & Alessi, A. (2003). An interview with Alito Alessi. Retrieved from http://www.danceability.com/malarkeyInterview.php.

Markula, P., & Silk, M. (2011). *Qualitative research for physical culture*. Basingstoke, UK: Palgrave Macmillan.

McWhorter, L. (1999). *Bodies and pleasures: Foucault and the politics of sexual normalization*. Bloomington: Indiana University Press.

Moore, C., & Yamamoto, K. (2012). *Beyond words: Movement observation and analysis*. New York: Routledge.

Novack, C. (1990). *Sharing the dance, contact improvisation and American culture*. Madison: University of Wisconsin Press.

Østern, T. P. (2009). *Meaning-making in the Dance Laboratory: Exploring dance improvisation with differently bodied dancers* (Doctoral dissertation). Teatterikorkeakoulu, Helsinki: Retrieved from https://helda.helsinki.fi/bitstream/handle/10138/33842/Acta_Scenica_23.pdf?sequence=1

Solidance Inclusive Recreation Society. (2015). *About*. Retrieved from www.solidance.ca

Stran, M., & Hardin, B. (2002). Teaching dance to children with ambulatory disabilities. *Teaching Elementary Physical Education, 13*(5), 33–35.

Whatley, S. (2007). Dance and disability: The dancer, the viewer and the presumption of difference. *Research in Dance Education, 8*, 5–25. doi:10.1080/14647890701272639

Withers, A. J. (2012). *Disability theory and politics*. Winnipeg, MB: Fernwood.

Zitomer, M. (2013). Creating space for every-body in dance education. *Physical & Health Education Journal, 79*(1), 18–21.

Zitomer, M., & Reid, G. (2011). To be or not to be—able to dance: Integrated dance and children's perceptions of dance ability and disability. *Research in Dance Education, 12*, 137–56.

CONCLUSION

Pirkko Markula and Marianne I. Clark

Throughout this book, the ballet body danced in diverse contemporary locations: in children's books, popular reality television shows, online workouts, and studios. Our book, concomitantly, revealed the many faces of ballet in Alberta: the young dancers who found solace in the local studios; the university students attending their ballet classes; the Albertan ballerinas performing in SYTYCD; and us, the authors, who all conducted our studies in Alberta.

This ballet body is primarily a female body—young, adolescent, student, professional, home exerciser, experiencing disability—who loves learning ballet technique, embraces performing with or without a tutu, competes to become Canada's favourite dancer, thinks of teaching ballet ethically, or hopes to gain leaner legs through ballet workouts. Unlike the world of professional ballet, women dominate the everyday ballet world: they choreograph, judge, write about, teach, and dance ballet. Additionally, women scholars, who are also dancers, choreographers, instructors, and performers, are the authors of the research that appears in this book.

The Multiplicity of Feminine Ballet Bodies

In this women's world, the lived and experienced ballet body differs
from the one appearing in the media. The ballet body in popular
television and women's magazines emphasizes what feminist
researchers (Adair, 1992; Foster, 1996; Oliver, 2005; Sherlock, 1993)
have identified as the ideal feminine ballet body: the willowy thin
body with long, lean legs. In television, as Markula (Chapter 2)
demonstrates, the feminine ballet body was also judged against
the formalist ideal of the Balanchine ballerina (Laemmli, 2015;
Morris, 2005): hyperflexible and technically able, yet not "sexy" or
expressive. While aware of the ideal ballerina's body, the dancers
in this book embraced other qualities such as the enjoyment of
dancing, building lasting friendships, or learning new skills in a
unique space where women can move without being sexualized. For
example, Clark (Chapter 4) demonstrates that adolescent girl dancers value learning new skills and expanding their movement the
most in their ballet class. The dance studio also provided a space in
which to explore and show off physicality without worrying about
appearing attractive or "sexy" to their peers. Similarly, dancers in
Millar's study (Chapter 5) described the strong friendships they
acquired through ballet, which contributed to their ongoing dance
involvement. For these dancers, negotiating the idealized ballet
body was only one aspect of their dance experiences. Teachers
also challenged dominant notions of the ballet body and reflected
on ethical ways to facilitate instruction for non-elite dancers. For
example, Acton and Eales (Chapter 7) created an inclusive pedagogy
to teach ballet in an integrated dance setting, and Vandekerkhove
(Chapter 6) thought actively about how a beginner ballet class
could be taught in ways that minimized disciplinary practices
while still allowing dancers to learn conventional ballet repertoire.
The dancers and their teachers were passionate about ballet, yet
they problematized many stereotypes and taken-for-granted ballet
practices. For some dancers, ballet became a tool to challenge the

idealized feminine body, social stereotypes of disability, or dominant ideas of what constitutes a dancing body.

At the same time, the recreational ballet class followed the traditional structure of professional ballet training (Aalten, 2004). For example, Davies (Chapter 1) describes how the children's books pictured ballet classes with barre exercises, centre work, and partnering in studios lined with mirrors, similar to professional ballet. Vandekerkhove (Chapter 6) shows that recreational beginner ballet classes in the university setting were conducted in a mirrored studio following the same structure. Participants in Clark's study (Chapter 4) referred to structured ballet classes that progressed steadily in complexity to increase dancers' technical proficiency. Through these practices, the traditional French movement vocabulary of ballet continues to live in contemporary ballet settings and is further borrowed to inform the ballet-inspired fitness workouts (Chapter 3). The dancers exhibited passion and dedication to dance akin to the professional ballet dancers, but did not encounter the same need to embrace "the culture of hardiness" (Wainwright & Turner, 2006) dominating the professional companies.

In summary, multiple forms of the ballet body appear throughout this book. The ballet body here is an energetic body capable of expressive movement and a disciplined body linked to dominant notions of ideal femininity and neoliberal citizenship. Its meanings shift with changing contexts. For example, the popular children's literature (Davies in Chapter 1), the fitness workouts (Markula and Clark in Chapter 3), and the popular reality shows (Markula in Chapter 2) reinforce the normative, feminine ballet body, whereas the ballet body in the local dance studio setting evades such fixed understandings through its capacity to contest common understandings of ability, body, and ballet. Therefore, the recreational ballet dancers are able to make multiple meanings in a dance context that, in many ways, continues to follow the traditions deriving from the romantic ballet and cemented in the neoclassism of Russian ballet. But, as the history of ballet demonstrates, choreographing and performing are created through the multiplicity of meanings invented by dancers in multiple settings.

In some sense, the contemporary feminine ballet body continues to be defined through the binary of the mediated, traditionally acceptable feminine body versus the lived ballet body of multiple meanings. This is, however, disrupted by the theoretical framing that challenges the division of the feminine ballet body being shaped only by the media or only through lived bodily experiences.

Multiple Understandings of the Ballet Body

The research presented in this book reflects a range of theoretical perspectives that illuminate multiple ways of understanding ballet and the ballet body. Expanding the previous critical cultural studies and psychoanalytic research, many of the authors employ a poststructuralist theoretical framework to examine how ballet is represented in media texts, but also how the ballet body is disciplined using the techniques of space, time, and movement practices. The works by Foucault and Deleuze provide useful tools to analyze the ballet body in action in contemporary neoliberal society. In this context, the ballet body easily becomes subject to the panoptic control of the invisible gaze that aligns it with the dominant ideals of our current society. For example, the neoliberal ideal of the thin, feminine body emerged through the practice of ballet in the local settings. It was constructed through individual engagement in proper diet and training in combination with the psychological construction of needing emotional relief and expressiveness. However, released from the historical binary between a technically skilful and expressive ballet body, the dancers enjoyed learning technical skills while acknowledging the importance of expressiveness in ballet.

Although the local ballet dancers focused on developing their own skills instead of the looks of the body, they acknowledged not striving for a professional career that, as they assumed, required increased body discipline. For example, dancers in Millar's study (Chapter 5) were aware that their physique and technical ability did not meet the demands of a professional career even if they had originally hoped to dance professionally. Nevertheless, these dancers wished to further their skill development and to remain dancing in a non-professional capacity to continue to enjoy dance and the social connections brought with it. Younger dancers in Clark's research (Chapter 4) also observed that significant disciplinary practices (e.g., dietary monitoring and increased training) would be required from professional ballet dancers, but they did not need to (or wish to) achieve this status to have satisfying and rewarding dance experiences. From a poststructuralist perspective, ballet dancers did not "escape" or transcend the dominant notions of the aesthetics of the ballet body, but they actively negotiated its meaning and purpose in their specific contexts. These findings, therefore, complicate the singular narrative of ballet as wholly oppressive. But while the dancers actively negotiated their personal meanings toward ballet, their physical prowess did not "saturate" them with liberatory agency (Banes, 1998) to step entirely outside of the dominant ballet discourse. For example, Vandekerkhove (Chapter 6) emphasizes the contextual, unfixed power relations that shape the ballet teacher's and dancers' practices and the importance of actively creating ethical teaching within these power relations. Together, this scholarship provides compelling impetus to continue work towards research that evokes social change.

Next Steps?

While we hope that this collection takes important steps towards presenting diverse faces of ballet and bringing forward the rich research conducted in Alberta, we acknowledge several limitations. First, while the focus was intentionally on ballet, many other dance forms play an important role in shaping how dance is understood in contemporary society. Furthermore, dance forms such as contemporary dance or contact improvisation have explicitly been identified as more liberating than ballet, and ballet is then deemed, dualistically, as an oppressive practice to women. Instead of reinforcing such a binary, future research can examine how diverse forms of dance exist in relationship to each other. After all, a number of the research participants as well as the authors of this collection participate in several dance forms that might inform and enrich each other.

Second, this book focused primarily on the representations and experiences of female ballet dancers. While there are several existing texts on male dancers' representations and experiences (e.g., Burt, 2007; Fisher & Shay, 2009; Gard, 2008; Risner, 2009), a comparative analysis of both gendered lenses can provide further valuable insights into the enduring lure of ballet. Davies's study (Chapter 1) already reveals differences in the way that children's ballet bodies are represented according to gender, and Markula's investigation of SYTYCD (Chapter 2) illustrates how female dancers are positioned in relation to male dancers as their "sexy" counterparts.

Finally, the historical overview of ballet reveals that it is a dance form with a predominant development and resonance in Western societies. Our research is based in Alberta, which as a part of Canada, draws its ballet heritage from the British Empire and the foundation of the British ballet examination board in 1920 when the Royal Academy of Dance (RAD) was established. The RAD has been crucial for the development of ballet in the British colonies such as Canada and elsewhere in the Commonwealth (Wulff, 2008). Yet ballet has expanded throughout the world with well-established ballet companies in Australia, China, Cuba, Hong Kong, Israel, Japan, New Zealand, South Africa, and South America (Wulff, 2008). An international research collaboration that maps possible differences and similarities between such diverse cultural contexts would reveal further multiplicities of ballet bodies.

As we conclude this book, we hope the vitality of the research that moves within these pages will continue to energize other researchers to engage with ballet and prompt expanded directions.

Each chapter in this book reveals new questions that may guide future inquiry. We hope that dance and physical cultural scholars will continue to explore innovative approaches to answering such questions, and to further interrogate how ballet bodies and ballet practices might be harnessed for social change. As Vandekerkhove (Chapter 6) and Acton and Eales (Chapter 7) demonstrate, power relations are dynamic, and small changes in instructional practice can result in changes in how bodies in studio spaces are experienced and understood. These authors provide an important opening in which to consider how social change can take place in local settings and how ballet can be practiced more inclusively.

In conclusion, we note how much energy and possibility the scholarly study of ballet, and dance in general, holds in this contemporary moment. This book, in small but important ways, answers calls for future approaches made earlier by dance scholars. For example, Banes (1998) made the compelling case for interrogating dance not in dualistic terms of oppression or liberation, but instead to consider the materiality of the dancing body, and the rigorous examination of the social and cultural (and political) production of dance and dancing bodies. The approaches taken in this book provide indications for ways in which we might continue to answer this call, through theoretical perspectives that refuse dualistic understandings and categorical identities, and through methodologies that accommodate the material body as a social force. We continue to write dance so that it continues to move those who study, practice, perform, and consume it.

References

Aalten, A. (2004). "The moment when it all comes together": Embodied experiences in ballet. *European Journal of Women's Studies, 11*(3), 263–76. doi:10.1177/1350506804044462

Adair, C. (1992). *Women and dance: Sylphs and sirens.* London: MacMillan.

Banes, S. (1998). *Dancing women: Female bodies on stage.* London: Routledge.

Burt, R. (2007). *The male dancer: Bodies, spectacle, sexualities.* London: Routledge.

Fisher, J., & Shay, A. (2009). *When men dance: Choreographing masculinities across borders.* New York: Oxford University Press.

Foster, S. L. (1996). The ballerina's phallic pointe. In S. L. Foster (Ed.), *Corporealities: Dancing, knowledge, culture and power* (1–24). London: Routledge.

Gard, M. (2008). *Men who dance: Aesthetics, athletics and art of masculinity.* New York: Peter Lang.

Laemmli, W. (2015). A case in pointe: Romance and regimentation at the New York City Ballet. *Technology and Culture, 56*(1), 1–27.

Morris, G. (2005). Balanchine's bodies. *Body & Society, 11,* 19–44.

Oliver, W. (2005). Reading the ballerina's body: Susan Bordo sheds light on Anastasia Volochkova and Heidi Guenther. *Dance Research Journal, 37,* 38–54.

Risner, D. (2009). *Stigma and perseverance in the lives of boys who dance: An empirical study of male identities in Western theatrical dance training.* Lewiston, NY: Edwin Mellen.

Sherlock, J. (1993). Dance and the culture of the body. In S. Scott & D. Morgan (Eds.), *Body matters: Essays on the sociology of the body* (35–46). Bristol, PA: Taylor & Francis.

Wainwright, S. P., & Turner, B. S. (2006). Varieties of habitus and the embodiment of ballet. *Qualitative Research, 6*(4), 535–58.

Wulff, H. (2008). Ethereal expression: Paradoxes of ballet as a global physical culture. *Ethnography, 9*(4), 518–35. doi:10.1177/1466138108096990

CONTRIBUTORS

KELSIE ACTON is a PHD student studying integrated dance, compulsory able-bodiedness, and time. Her research is supported by a SSHRC Doctoral Scholarship. She has been practicing integrated dance since 2010 as a dancer, rehearsal director, teacher, and choreographer. Kelsie is one of the founding members and co-artistic director of CRIPSiE (Collaborative Radically Integrated Performers Society in Edmonton) and the instructional co-ordinator of Solidance Inclusive Recreation Society.

MARIANNE I. CLARK is a postdoctoral research fellow in the School of Human Development and Movement Studies at the University of Waikato, New Zealand, as well as a contemporary dancer. Marianne's research focuses on the body, girls' and women's dance and physical activity experiences, and the increasing intersections of technology, bodily movement, and health. She draws upon qualitative research methods and poststructuralist theory to examine the moving body's capacity to change and destabilize dominant understandings of health, gender, and the ideal feminine body.

KATE Z. DAVIES holds a PHD from the University of Alberta, as well as an MA with a specialization in early childhood physical activity and sport psychology. Her interest in children's literature, as a medium through which meanings of the moving body are circulated during childhood, underpinned her doctoral research. More specifically, this research problematized physical activity, represented in children's picture books, as a space that reproduces norms and restricts our understanding of the children's bodies and their capacity for movement and play.

LINDSAY EALES is a choreographer, instructor, performer, and scholar who explores integrated dance, disability, madness, and social justice. She is a PHD candidate in the Faculty of Physical Education and Recreation at the University of Alberta. Her work has been published in journals including *Adapted Physical Activity Quarterly*, *Leisure/Loisir*, and *Emotions, Space, and Society*. Her PHD work uses research-creation to explore mad politics, aesthetics, and mad-accessible practices through dance. She is supported by the Vanier Canada Graduate Scholarship (SSHRC). Lindsay is a founder and co-artistic director of CRIPSiE (Collaborative Radically Integrated Performers Society in Edmonton) and the programming director of Solidance Inclusive Recreation Society.

PIRKKO MARKULA is a professor of sociocultural studies of physical activity at the University of Alberta. Her research interests include social analyses of dance, exercise, and sport in which she has employed several theoretical lenses ranging from critical, cultural studies research to Foucault and Deleuze. She is also a contemporary dancer and choreographer. She is the co-author, with Michael Silk, of *Qualitative Research for Physical Culture* (Routledge, 2011); co-author, with Richard Pringle, of *Foucault, Sport and Exercise: Power, Knowledge and Transforming the Self* (Routledge, 2006).

CAROLYN MILLAR began dance at a young age, training in a competitive studio, ballet school, and later university modern dance group. She continues to dance and has worked as an instructor for a dance studio specializing in early childhood development. Today, Carolyn continues to work to enrich childhood education through outdoor recreation and environmental education. Carolyn has a BSC in kinesiology and an MA in physical education and recreation, both from the University of Alberta.

JODIE VANDEKERKHOVE is a professional artist with extensive training and education in the field of dance, holding a BFA and a MA, each with a focus on dance. She has danced professionally for various choreographers and has performed for the Jen Mesch Dance Conspiracy, KO Dance project, and Mile Zero Dance. Jodie has most recently been a presenter for the TEDx Garneau Women event. Jodie has a passion for teaching dance and presently is a sessional dance instructor at Concordia University of Edmonton and the University of Alberta. She is also the outreach co-ordinator for Mile Zero Dance.

INDEX

analysis of their use in popular
fitness regimes, 57–64, 73

assessment of their applicability to
fitness regimes, 64–67

and body aesthetics, 68–69

popular interest in for fitness,
49–50

project sampling strategy, 53–54

safety concern for non-dancers, 62,
63, 64

use of dance experts in, 67–68

visible aspects of, 54–55

barre

as part of popular fitness workouts,
60–61, 64

portrayed in children's literature,
14

students' reaction to, 138

use of in integrated dance, 163,
164, 165

Barron, Corynne

development and work in popular
dance, 39, 40–41, 42

face of on *So You Think You Can
Dance*, 34, 35–36, 37, 38

beauty, 17, 21–22

beginner ballet

achieving a tutu, 17, 18

and disciplinary techniques in
teaching, 129–36

and discipline, 14–15

importance of teacher in, 127,
147–48

popularity of, 127–28

response to space allocated for,
137–40

students' attitude toward learning
movement, 143–47

students' attitude toward uniform,
139–40

students' pleasure in, 148

students' response to mirrors,
138–39

students' view of time allocation
during, 140–43

being in-between, 96

Bertram, Allie

development and work in popular
dance, 38–40, 41, 42

face of on *So You Think You Can
Dance*, 34, 35, 36–38

body aesthetics, 68–69

body awareness, 35–36, 88–89, 91, 112

body consciousness, 139

body dissatisfaction, 103

Bourne, Matthew, xx

brain-compatible dance, 161

BrainDance, 161–62

Bryant, Anthony, 29

Camargo, Marie, xviii

Candoco, 152, 155

careful body, 91–92

Cheeseman, Sean, 45n6

children's literature

analysis of ballet in, 12–20

assessment of portrayal of ballet
in, 21–23

methodology used in analysis of,
11–12

review of scholarship on, 4–9

concrete faces, 43

contact improvisation, 154–57

contemporary dance. *See* recreational
contemporary dance

corps de ballet, xxi–xxii

CRIPSiE (Collaborative Radically
Integrated Performers Society
in Edmonton), 153

Cunningham, Merce, 121

DanceAbility, 155

dance in movies, 45n1

Dancing Wheels, 152

Dancing with the Stars, 27, 28, 45n2

defacialization, 44

Diaghilev, Sergei, xxxn1

in history of ballet, xvii–xviii, xix
and language of movement, 133–34
and reality contestants failing at,
29
teaching to disabled dancers,
156–57. *See also* disciplinary
techniques; inclusive technique
therapeutic language, 162
Tookey, Stacey, 39, 40
training
appreciation of difficulty of ballet,
104–05
emphasis of on *So You Think You
Can Dance*, 41
focus of reality tv dance shows
on, 29
negative experiences of, 101, 102–03
portrayal of in children's literature,
16
positive experiences of, 104–06

recreational dancers' appreciation
of hard work, 89–90, 91, 113–14
representation of in children's
literature, 8
truth-effect, 9–10, 11, 21, 82
tutus
feminist view of, 30
history of, xxi, xxiii
as sign of accomplishment, 12, 17,
18, 20
in *So You Think You Can Dance*,
37, 42
as symbol of ballet, 3

uniform, 139–40

Wall, Travis, 30
Williams, Allison, 62

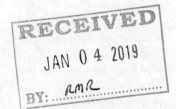

Other Titles from The University of Alberta Press

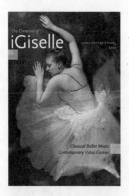

The Creation of iGiselle
Classical Ballet Meets Contemporary Video Games
Nora Foster Stovel, Editor

Romantic ballet meets artificial intelligence to change the tragic narrative, allowing for possible "feminine endings."

Game Plan
A Social History of Sport in Alberta
Karen L. Wall

Patterns and layers of sport history emerge as almost-forgotten stories of Alberta's marginalized populations surface.

Not Drowning But Waving
Women, Feminism and the Liberal Arts
Susan Brown, Jeanne Perreault, Jo-Ann Wallace & Heather Zwicker, Editors

A welcome progress report on the variety of feminisms at work in academe and beyond.

More information at www.uap.ualberta.ca